COULD IT BE TRUE?

COULD IT BE TRUE?

ALLAN ZULLO

*This book is dedicated to my grandson
Danny Allan Manausa, who, coincidentally,
was born on the day that I finished this manuscript.*

Contents

Introduction: What a Coincidence!

Have you ever thought of someone for no reason at all and suddenly that person calls you on the phone? Have you ever been on a vacation far from home and unexpectedly bumped into a friend you know from school?

These are examples of a coincidence—two events that happen at the same time, apparently by accident yet, astonishingly enough, having some sort of connection. Many people believe coincidences are caused by fate, destiny, luck, or serendipity. Whatever the cause, coincidences all have one trait in common: They are amazing surprises.

In this book, you will read about incredible coincidences that are either strange twists of fate, unbelievable examples of luck, or wondrous happenings of serendipity. Although these stories are based on true accounts from around the world, dialogue and several scenes have been dramatized and names and places have been changed to protect people's privacy.

Who knows? Maybe when you finish reading this book, you'll be awed by something surprising. Now wouldn't that be a coincidence?

Painted by the Hand of Fate

"You never know what you'll find in an antiques store," said Dana Warden. "That's what makes it so much fun to browse."

"You mean finding something like this?" asked her fourteen-year-old daughter, Molly, holding up an old-fashioned ravioli cutter.

"Exactly," her mother confirmed.

Molly put the ravioli cutter down and continued to worm her way through all the clutter, not looking for anything in particular. But among all the interesting items in the cramped shop—the antique porcelain, the knickknacks, the hand-crafted furniture, the rusty tools—Molly was about to find the one thing that would forever change the lives of everyone in her family.

Unlike most kids her age, Molly enjoyed tagging along with her parents whenever they went antiquing. Her father, Tom, who worked for a company that restored old buildings, had taught her an appreciation for furniture and objects that were crafted decades, even centuries, ago.

"There's something cool about running your fingers across a pine china cabinet made before the Civil War," she once explained to her friends. "It wasn't made in a factory. It was made with pride by someone who really cared about his work. When I admire an old piece, I try to picture who that person was, why he made the object, and especially who used it. I like to build stories in my mind and imagine what life was like back then." Her friends nodded politely and then changed the subject to something more current, like the newest Hanson CD.

On this particular day, Molly and her parents had spent a half hour rummaging through the quaint antiques store. Nineteenth-century farm equipment, much of it worn and dusty, dangled on hooks above a jumble of pine, oak, and walnut chests, dressers, and chairs.

"Come on, girls," shouted Tom from the front of the store. "Let's grab a bite to eat."

"I'm all for that," Molly agreed. As she walked past a large dresser, her eyes fell on a painting stuck behind a brass lamp and a three-legged bookcase. The picture, set in a simple wood frame, showed a charming Victorian house nestled among flowering dogwoods. She pulled out the oil-on-canvas and studied it carefully.

A wraparound porch trimmed in white girdled the large, rust-colored, three-story house. The slate-gray roof featured four gables, each with a shutter-bordered window. At the front of the house rose a windowed turret that peaked into a spire above the gables. An oval-shaped stained-glass window topped the white carved front door. A stone walkway led from the front door down a hill adorned with eye-catching pink and white dogwoods. Two white-painted stone benches stood under four orange-red crepe myrtle trees.

Molly didn't know much about paintings and was hardly an art lover, but this piece intrigued her. The artist had created the scene in such exquisite detail that Molly was sure the house had really existed. In the lower right-hand corner of the canvas, she saw a signature scribbled in black: "Sandler '39."

I wonder who lived there? Molly thought. *It must have been someone very interesting, perhaps a poet or an inventor. Or maybe a cold-hearted banker who was so mean that . . . no, not this house. It's too pretty. I'll bet a handsome young man built it for his new bride, who—*

"Molly, are you coming?" Dana called from the other side of the store.

"Mom, Dad. Come here, please."

When they walked over to her, Molly showed them the painting. "What do you think?" she asked.

"It's rather nice," Dana replied.

"Looks like a classic Victorian," Tom said.

"I don't know why, but I like this painting a lot," bubbled Molly. "Can I buy it?"

"You're a big girl," Tom told her. "It's up to you—assuming it's reasonably priced—although I'm not quite sure why you'd want it."

"I just have a good feeling about it, like nice things happened there. Does that sound crazy?"

"Not for you," Tom retorted with a wink.

Molly brought the painting over to the owner of the shop.

After examining the canvas with one eye, the owner said, "Twenty bucks ought to do it."

"Do you know anything about the painting?" Molly asked.

"Not really. It came from an estate auction over in Centerville a year ago. Typical story. A couple are married for fifty years, she dies, and then the kids ship him off to a retirement home and get rid of most everything." Glaring into Molly's green eyes, the woman waggled her index finger at the auburn-haired girl and growled, "Don't you do that to your parents when they get old."

"I won't. Um, will you take ten dollars for it?"

"The frame is worth more than that, young lady. Tell you what. Split the difference and it's yours."

Molly grinned and declared, "Deal."

She opened up her backpack, then muttered, "Uh-oh. Um, Mom, I've only got ten dollars. Can you—"

"Don't worry about it," Tom said, and he handed the shop owner fifteen dollars.

"Thanks, Dad! I love you."

Smiling at his daughter, Tom said, "Do you love me enough to help me clean out the garage this afternoon?"

She looked at the painting and then at her father. "You got me," she groaned.

Molly walked out of the shop, carrying what she thought was just a pretty picture. Nothing about the painting hinted that this canvas had been painted by the hand of fate.

Later that day, Molly hung the painting in her room next to the window by her bed. The colors on the canvas complemented the lavender walls, her creamy comforter, and the soft yellow-and-pink Oriental rug that covered much of the dark-stained oak floor. Her room, like the rest of the Wardens' century-old restored house, had its share of antique furnishings, so the picture fit in perfectly with the decor.

Shortly after Molly bought her "feel good" painting, life for the Wardens turned terribly sour. First, Dana lost her job as the assistant manager of a women's apparel shop when the store went out of business. "Being out of work is bad enough," Dana complained at the dinner table when she broke the bad news to her family. "But even worse, I'm owed fifteen hundred dollars in back pay, which I'll probably never get."

"Don't worry, sweetheart," consoled Tom. "Our company is busier than ever. I can put in for overtime until you find another job. With your work experience and contacts, that phone will be ringing off the hook with job offers."

"Mrs. Flanagan is always asking me to help out at her flower shop," said Molly. "I'll call her up and—"

Dana cut her off. "No, Molly. You're too young to work. When you're an adult, you'll be working for the rest of your life. Enjoy being a kid for as long as you can. We'll manage."

But life soon became more difficult than the Wardens ever imagined. Just two weeks after Dana lost her job, Tom suffered a serious injury. He was restoring a downtown hotel when the scaffolding he was standing on suddenly collapsed. Tom plunged to the sidewalk nearly twenty feet below. He broke several bones in his back and had to stay in bed for three months.

Unfortunately, Tom's painful back problems persisted, and he was unable to return to the restoration work he loved so much. Although insurance covered the medical bills and some other expenses, the Wardens had to spend most of their savings—including Molly's college fund—just to survive. The family was living on Dana's meager income as a sales clerk at a mall department store. Meanwhile, Molly worked ten hours a week at the florist's shop after school to help out.

One night at an unusually quiet dinner, Dana asked Molly, "So, are you and Jacob going to the spring dance next week?"

Molly tossed her fork into the mashed potatoes, looked up with tears welling in her eyes, and snapped, "No. I don't have anything new to wear, and it doesn't matter anyway because Jacob and I broke up." She balled up her napkin, fired it at the meatloaf, and fled the table, crying uncontrollably.

Molly dashed up to her room, slammed the door, and dove on top of her bed, burying her head in her pillow. Moments later, she heard a knock. "Honey, I'm so sorry," said Dana. "I didn't know. Do you want to talk about it?"

"Not now," Molly choked between sobs. After crying enough tears to soak her pillow, Molly sat up and found herself staring at the painting of the Victorian house that graced her bedroom wall.

"I had a good feeling about you when I bought you," she muttered to the picture. "But ever since I brought you home, my family and I have had one rotten thing after another happen to us." Angrily reaching for the painting, she ripped it off the wall and flung it across the room. "You're bad luck!"

The picture slammed into her desk, toppling over a stack of *Southern Living* magazines. Molly stormed over to her desk. She picked up the painting and raised it over her head. She was ready to smash it against her bedpost when she noticed that one of the fallen magazines had opened to a page headlined THE PIONEER OF BACK REPAIR.

Molly put down the painting and picked up the magazine. The article described a physician in Birmingham, Alabama, who had discovered a revolutionary new procedure to help victims of back injury. "Maybe he can help Daddy!" Molly thought out loud.

A few weeks later, the Wardens—full of hope for the first time since Tom's accident—drove the 150 miles to Birmingham to meet with the doctor. After a thorough examination and a review of Tom's X rays, the surgeon announced, "I think we can get rid of your back pain, Tom. You probably won't be able to do much physical work, but you'll lead an otherwise normal life again."

The Wardens were ecstatic and celebrated with a big lunch at a nice restaurant—a luxury they had denied themselves for months. "I might not be able to restore old buildings anymore, but without my back pain, I'll find a good job," Tom pledged to his family.

Rather than drive home on the interstate, Molly convinced her parents to take the scenic route with a quick side trip to see the Carlton Covered Bridge. She had read about the bridge in the same *Southern Living* issue that carried the back surgeon's story.

The rickety tin-roofed bridge stretched over the Peace River. As the Wardens' car slowly eased across the warped boards, the sixty-year-old span moaned and popped. Molly looked through the bridge's crisscrossed timber sides at the green water moving slowly below. "Ooh, this is so awesome," she marveled. "I've never gone through a covered bridge before."

When they emerged from the other side, they spotted a

lanky, elderly man in a baseball cap, white shirt, and dark pants. He was bent over the open hood of a car that had wisps of steam fluttering from its engine.

Tom pulled over. "Car trouble?"

"My dang radiator sprung a leak," the man replied.

"Can we give you a lift?" asked Tom.

"Much obliged," said the man, tipping his cap. "I live only a couple of miles from here."

With some effort, the man climbed into the backseat next to Molly. He took off his cap and introduced himself. "I'm Olin Milsap. My daddy helped build this bridge back in 1935. I had a small hand in it, too. He accidentally dropped his favorite hammer into the river, and he told a bunch of us boys that he'd pay fifty cents to whoever found it. That was a lot of money to me back then, so I ran down to the river, took off my clothes, and dove into the water. Don't you know, I found that hammer and collected my fifty cents."

A few minutes later, the Wardens dropped Mr. Milsap off at his residence—a high school that had been converted into a retirement home. "Thank you, kind folks," he said with a tip of his cap. "To get back on the main road, go another two blocks and turn right."

As they drove off, Dana said, "What a pleasant man. I loved his story. Didn't you, Molly?"

Molly didn't answer. Her eyes were glued to a Victorian house they were passing. Her heart pounded wildly with unbridled surprise. "Stop the car! Stop the car!" she shouted.

Tom slammed on the brakes, fearful that he had struck some small animal. "What? What?" he asked worriedly.

"Look!" shouted Molly, pointing to the house.

"So?" Tom replied. "I see a Victorian house. Am I missing something?"

"My gosh, Tom, you are!" Dana exclaimed. "That's the house in the painting in Molly's room!"

From the backseat, Molly reached up and squeezed her parents' shoulders. "The wraparound porch, the turret, the four gables, the stained-glass window over the front door," she said excitedly. "They're all here. Even the stone walkway and benches. It's exactly like in my painting! Come on, let's go talk to the owner."

"Honey, you can't just barge into somebody's house," said Tom.

Molly pressed her case. "Maybe they lost the painting. Maybe it means something to them. Besides, I'm dying to know who lives there. Come on. Please?"

Moments later, the Wardens knocked at the front door, which was answered by a stylishly dressed woman in her sixties. "Please forgive the interruption," said Dana, "but we were passing by when we noticed that your house looks like one in a painting that my daughter owns. She wanted to meet the people who live here."

"Please, come in." The woman greeted them with a sweeping gesture of her hand. "My name is Betsy Sandler."

"Sandler?" Molly gasped. "That's the name of the person who painted the picture. Are you the artist?"

"Oh, heavens no. I can't even paint a wall let alone a picture. But I know who did paint it—my husband's sister, Cece. I can't believe it still exists."

"It very nearly was destroyed," said Molly. "It's in my closet right now."

After serving the Wardens lemonade, Betsy sat down and told them the story of the painting. "This house was built for my husband's parents back at the turn of the century. My husband, Joe, and his older sister, Cece, grew up here. Cece was a wonderful artist. She knew she would be leaving the area when she got married in 1939, so she painted a picture of the house and took it with her as a reminder when she moved to Centerville with her husband.

"She died about two years ago, after her fifty-first wedding anniversary. Her children convinced her husband to sell virtually everything and move back here to the retirement home down the street. Poor Olin. He's never been the same since Cece's death."

"Olin?" said Molly. "What's his last name?"

"Milsap."

"This is getting weird!" Molly declared. "There are too many coincidences. We just dropped Olin Milsap off at the home a few minutes ago. We never would've seen this house if we hadn't met him. And we never would've met him if we hadn't visited the wooden bridge. And we wouldn't have visited the bridge if we hadn't seen the doctor, and we wouldn't have seen the doctor if I hadn't thrown the painting and knocked over a stack of magazines and . . . oh, it's just amazing!"

It wasn't nearly as amazing as what happened shortly after Betsy's husband, Joe, arrived home. During the course of his conversation with the Wardens, Joe mentioned that he owned a mail-order business that sold antique items and reproductions to contractors and people who restore old houses and buildings.

"Restoration?" yelped Tom. "That's my craft—or it was until I hurt my back."

"Really? I'm looking for a manager to help run the business. Are you interested?"

Tom stood straight up, ignoring the pain in his back, and declared, "I'm your man!"

When the deliriously happy Wardens returned home that night, the first thing Molly did was run up to her room, dig the painting out of the closet, and put it back on the wall.

CF8WRK4U

Seeing the exit sign for Belvidere, Malik Jones eased his car into the far right lane of the highway. "It'll be good to be home, won't it, Chantelle?"

His girlfriend and neighbor, Chantelle Morris, who was riding home with Malik from college for Thanksgiving break, nodded. "Mmmm. I can't wait to dig into that roast turkey and stuffing and mashed potatoes and gravy. I can almost smell Mama's sweet potato pie."

Malik licked his lips at the thought. "I'm looking forward to real home cooking, too—not the slop they serve in the dorm cafeteria. My dogs wouldn't eat the mystery meat they serve there."

When a red light stopped them at a busy intersection, Malik let out an approving whistle. "Would you look at that?" He pointed to a polished purple car rumbling alongside them. "It's a 1958 Edsel in mint condition. Very cool."

"That's one of the ugliest cars I've ever seen," said Chantelle with a laugh. "The front grille looks like a toilet seat, and those wide wings on the back belong on a vulture. The worst is the color. Purple! Ugh!"

"The Edsel was a classic—a classic failure. I learned about it in marketing class. The car was built by Ford and turned out to be a real lemon. It had all sorts of problems with the power steering, oil leaks, and stuck hoods and trunks. So few Edsels were bought that Ford lost about three thousand dollars on each car. It would've been cheaper for the company to have given away a new Mercury to every Edsel buyer instead of selling them an Edsel."

"If the car was such a loser, why would anyone be seen in one—especially a purple one?" asked Chantelle.

"Edsels are so tacky that they're kind of neat. And they're pretty rare, too. Oh, well, we'll probably never see a car like that again."

Chantelle patted the seat of Malik's old Chevy. "This car is good enough for me. It got us home for Thanksgiving. It was so sweet of your dad to buy you this car."

"Don't I know it," Malik agreed. "Six years ago we were living in a tenement down that street over there. Then Dad got his master's degree in marketing and landed that great job at Sandstrom's. Now we live in a nice neighborhood, and he can afford to put me through school and give me a car. He's great."

Malik pulled his Chevy up to the curb in front of Chantelle's house. "Well, here we are," he said. "I'll help you unload."

As he opened the door, he heard a car roaring down the street toward him. "What's his hurry?" Then he noticed the telltale toilet-seat-shaped front grille. "Not another Edsel?" But as the car got closer, Malik realized it was the same purple Edsel that had been at the intersection a few minutes earlier. This time it looked like it was aiming for him.

"Geez, he's awfully close to the curb," Malik said. "Oh, no! He's going to hit the door!" Malik dove into the backseat, slamming the door behind him. The Edsel zoomed by and, with tires squealing, turned at the next corner and disappeared into the twilight.

"Malik, are you okay?" asked Chantelle, rushing over to the car. "That was a close call. He missed hitting the door by inches. You could've been killed!"

As Malik scrambled out of the car, he shook his head angrily. "Did you see who that maniac was?"

Chantelle shook her head. "I couldn't tell if it was a man or a woman. I'm guessing it's a man because a woman wouldn't drive like that. And she certainly wouldn't be caught dead in a purple Edsel."

Malik laughed. The two then unloaded her gear without further incident. After saying hello to her folks, Malik asked them, "Have you ever seen a purple Edsel around here?"

Chantelle's parents shook their heads. "I haven't seen one in years," said her mother. Playfully jabbing an elbow into her husband's side, she added, "With our habit of buying lemons, it's a good thing Willis wasn't old enough back in the late fifties or he would've bought the first Edsel off the assembly line."

Malik kissed Chantelle good-bye and headed the eight blocks to his house. He didn't think anything more about the purple Edsel until Thanksgiving night. Still stuffed from the huge afternoon meal, he and his dad, Jarrett, decided to take a walk in the crisp air.

As they stepped out the front door, they spotted a car

slowly drive up their cul-de-sac, turn around, and head back. "What kind of car is that?" asked Jarrett.

Malik squinted in the blackness, barely able to make out the boxy frame on the dark-colored car. Then the car passed under a streetlight several houses away, and Malik made out the widespread, winged rear-end of an Edsel. A purple one.

"It's that Edsel again! Dad, have you ever seen a purple Edsel in the neighborhood?"

"The only Edsel I've seen was in an auto show a couple of years ago. Why?"

"It's odd, but ever since I hit town, I've been seeing a purple Edsel. It darn near tore the door off my car when I opened it at Chantelle's. It's like the car is haunting me. I'd really like to know who the driver is."

The next day, Malik was driving toward Chantelle's house, thinking about the plans they had made to see friends. Suddenly he slammed on his brakes as a streak of purple burst out from a side street. It was the Edsel. The car pulled out just a few yards ahead of him and turned to the right. His Chevy shuddered as its screeching tires laid a streak of rubber. Malik took a deep breath and gritted his teeth in anger. "That's it, you jerk. I'm going after you!"

He put his foot on the accelerator and quickly caught up to the Edsel, which seemed to slow down as if waiting for Malik. The Edsel then stayed at the neighborhood's thirty-mile-per-hour speed limit. Rather than turn down Chantelle's street, Malik continued to follow the Edsel as it entered a commercial area where the streets were much busier. *I'll wait for the next light to turn red, and then I'll get out and learn who this guy is*, Malik thought. *I wonder what his game is. At the very least, I'll*

23

get his license number. Looking at the plate, he memorized the numbers and letters: CF8WRK4U.

The one time in his life Malik hoped for a red light, he didn't get one. They drove through three green traffic signals in a row. Still, the Edsel never broke the speed limit or drove erratically. It only turned once, heading downtown. *Hey, I've got all day, buddy*, Malik thought. Another turn, another green light.

A minute later, they arrived at a busy intersection just as the light turned from green to yellow. "All right! This is it! He's got to stop now!" Malik said out loud. But the Edsel sped through the intersection as the light changed to red. Caught off guard, Malik had to stop at the light. "Darn it!" he shouted, slamming his fist into the steering wheel. "He's getting away!" The Edsel slowed down when it reached the other side of the intersection and then turned left down an alley and disappeared among a row of tenements.

After the light turned green, Malik crossed the intersection and turned at the alley, hoping the Edsel was waiting for him in this bizarre cat-and-mouse chase. But the purple car was nowhere to be seen. Only then did Malik become aware of exactly where he was.

His car had stopped in the same garbage-strewn alley where he had grown up. He stared sullenly at the four-story apartment building that had been his childhood home. Soot from nearby factories had caked the brown brick with unsightly streaks of black. The fire escapes were rusted, and several windows were cracked. Nothing had changed, except that the building looked even more run-down. The only improvement was a chain-link fence enclosing the backyard.

Malik thought about all the stickball games he had played in the alley and how many times he'd had to hide when gangs invaded the area. He gazed at the building, wondering how many kids would ever make it out of there; how many would cling to dreams rather than the false hope offered by gang-bangers; how many would be as lucky as he was. He had parents who had scrimped and saved for a better life and had demanded that he study and stay out of trouble so that he would never have to live in a place like this again.

His thoughts were interrupted by a high-pitched scream. Malik jumped out of the car and scanned the area.

"Help me! Someone please help!"

Malik looked up and saw a woman's head sticking out of the third-floor window. "I'm trapped in the bathroom. I can't get out!" she screamed. "The doorknob fell out, and the door is locked."

Malik almost laughed. Then he saw the look of panic on her face. "I've got my two grandbabies in the kitchen and a boiling pot on the stove! Please, please, get help!"

"I'll be right up," yelled Malik.

"No, get help. My apartment is locked. You'll never get in."

"Oh, yes, I will. Stay calm. I'm coming right up."

"But you don't know what apartment I'm in!" the woman shouted. Malik paid no attention to her. The back gate was locked, so he climbed over the fence and opened the back door.

Malik dashed up the three flights of stairs and into the hallway. He ran to the second door on the right and tried to open it, but it was bolted shut. He pounded on the door, hoping that one of the children inside would unlock it for him. But

25

after a minute, it was clear no one was going to open the door from the inside.

He reached into his billfold and took out a credit card. He slipped it between the door and the doorjamb by the lock and carefully wiggled it until he heard a click. But the door still wouldn't open. There was a second lock on the doorknob itself.

I need something long and thin, Malik thought. *I wonder . . .* He felt along the baseboard to the left of the door. His fingers found a crack. He yanked hard and pulled apart a six-inch section of the wood. A small piece of sturdy wire from a coat hanger fell out. Malik couldn't believe it was still there after all those years.

He inserted the wire into the hole in the middle of the doorknob and expertly moved it until the lock sprung. Then he turned the knob, and the door swung open.

Malik rushed into the kitchen, but he didn't see any children there. A pot of soup was boiling over, splashing onto the floor. He shoved the pot off the burner and turned off the flame.

Next he ran to the bathroom door and pounded on it. "I'm here."

"How did you get in the apartment?" the trapped woman cried.

"I'll tell you later, after I help you get out. Just do exactly as I say. This bathroom door is very tricky. First, get down on your knees. Now put your index finger in the hole where the rod to the knob used to be. You'll feel a little lever on the left side of the hole. Push it in, and at the same time, slip your other hand under the door and lift it. Then shove the door with your shoulder. It should open."

The woman followed Malik's instructions perfectly. Within seconds, the door opened. She staggered out and gave Malik a quick hug. Then she scurried around the apartment, looking for her little grandchildren. She found them behind the couch. They told her that when she got trapped in the bathroom and started to scream, they became scared and hid.

After showering them with hugs, kisses, and reassurances that everything was fine, the woman told Malik, "I'm baby-sitting. This is my daughter's apartment, and I didn't know how to get out when the doorknob broke. How did you know what to do? How did you break into the apartment? How did you even know which apartment it was?"

"As soon as I heard you screaming from the window and telling me about the doorknob, I knew which apartment to go to," he explained. "You see, I used to live here when I was younger, so I know all about that doorknob."

"Oh, my word," she gasped. "Of all the people in this city, you just happened to be the one to come at the time I needed your help."

"That's an amazing coincidence, isn't it? Everyone in my family learned how to get out if we had a problem with the bathroom door. I was able to break into your apartment because my older brother taught me how to get in without a key. We hid a piece of wire in the baseboard and used it to spring the lock on the knob of the front door. The wire was still in its hiding place."

"You are an angel. Where do you live now?"

"In Grandview Heights."

"But that's clear across town. How did you end up over here?"

"It's a long story. You don't know anyone who drives a purple Edsel, do you, Ms., um . . ."

"Oh, I'm sorry," the woman said, extending her hand. "My name is Violet Plum. My mother had a sense of humor and a thing for the color purple."

"My name is Malik Jones. Purple seems to be the color of the day. I'm sure glad I could help you." He looked at his watch. "Uh-oh, I'm in trouble. I was supposed to be at my girlfriend's house thirty minutes ago. I better run."

"I still think you're an angel sent here to help me."

"I'm no angel, but I wonder if maybe I wasn't directed here."

Later, when Malik told Chantelle what had happened, he asked her, "Doesn't it strike you as really bizarre that a purple car suddenly appears in my life and then I tail it, only to lose it right at my old house at the exact moment some lady needs my help in my former apartment?"

"That's more than odd," she replied. "It's definitely beyond coincidence."

"I wonder who was driving that Edsel."

"Do you remember the license plate number?"

"Yeah, CF8WRK4U."

"Hmm, that sounds like one of those vanity license plates that has letters and numbers spelling out a name or a message."

Chantelle wrote down the Edsel's license plate and studied the combination of numbers and letters. A minute later, she triumphantly shouted, "Ah-hah! I've got it. The 'C' stands for 'see.' An 'F' in front of an eight sounds like 'fate.'"

"Oh, my gosh," said Malik, "now I understand. It says, 'See fate work for you'!"

The Money Bag

"Mama," cried Kayla Templeton. "Where are we going to live?"

The fourteen-year-old girl sat on the sun-parched ground outside the crumbling five-unit apartment building. She wrapped her arms around her tucked-up knees and sobbed.

Kayla; her twelve-year-old sister, Amy; and her mother, Jan, were being evicted from their apartment because the building had been sold. The new owner had given everyone thirty days' notice to leave before he tore down the building. The other four families had found new places. But the Templetons weren't that lucky.

Jan had moved the family from Missouri to Georgia two months earlier to join her husband, Rocky, who had started a new construction job. But a few weeks after their arrival, Rocky had been injured in a traffic accident. He had suffered severe head injuries and multiple broken bones and had been in the hospital ever since.

It seemed as though life for the Templetons couldn't get

any harder. They had no place to live and little money—not nearly enough for the first and last month's rent plus security deposit required by most landlords. Rocky was in the hospital with mounting medical bills. Jan, who had never graduated from high school, had a part-time job as a waitress, but she barely earned enough to pay for groceries. They had yet to make friends and had no relatives nearby. . . . But the family refused to leave town with Rocky still in the hospital.

Seeing Kayla cry, Amy burst into tears as the new owner dumped the last of the Templetons' possessions in the scraggly, weed-covered yard.

Jan threw her arms around her girls and tried to comfort them. "I know things seem bleak now, but they'll get better. We'll find a place to live, I promise."

"Are we going to have to stay in a shelter?" asked Amy.

"Not if I can help it. We Templetons don't seek handouts. Now listen to me. I don't want you to say a word to Daddy about this, okay? We don't need to put this burden on him. He's suffered enough and needs to get well."

"But what are we going to do?" asked Kayla.

"You like the outdoors, right? So we're going to camp out at the state park while I look for a place to live. It'll be fun."

"What you really mean is we're going to be living out of our van," Kayla moaned.

"We're homeless!" wailed Amy.

"Call it what you want," said Jan. "I prefer the term car-camping. I promise you, things will get better."

"Yeah," groused Kayla. "That's only because things can't get much worse."

The Templetons had left most of their belongings and

furniture back in Missouri, hoping to earn enough money to afford a better home before moving all their things. Now they crammed the meager contents of their condemned apartment in the back of the van, paid a visit to the hospital to see Rocky, and then drove to the campground at Slick Rock State Park.

For ten dollars a day, the family had their own small camping area with running water and a grill for cooking. The bathroom and showers were only a short distance away.

"Let's make the best of our situation," Jan told her girls. "After all, people go to state parks for fun. So take advantage of this. There's a swimming hole not far from here and lots of trails for hiking."

Jan went to buy a newspaper so she could check the want ads for apartments and new job openings. Meanwhile, Kayla and Amy, dressed in T-shirts and shorts, grabbed some towels and followed the trail to Slick Rock Falls. It was a popular spot for families because the falls made a natural water slide. A stream spilled over a forty-foot-wide, twelve-foot-high smooth boulder into a crystal-clear pool. Kids and adults sat in the stream on top of the boulder and let the water carry them down the boulder and into the pool.

For the rest of the afternoon, the two girls forgot about their troubles and slipped and slid off Slick Rock Falls on their backs and bellies. They returned to the campsite feeling more upbeat than they had all week. That evening, the Templetons ate well, grilling cheeseburgers and stuffing themselves with food that would otherwise spoil because they no longer had a refrigerator. When night fell, the girls and their mother lay on the picnic table and gazed up at the stars.

Suddenly a meteor streaked across the sky, leaving a

brilliant bluish-green tail. "Oh, a shooting star! Make a wish!" Amy squealed.

"I wish for Daddy to get well," said Jan.

"I wish we could find a nice place to live," said Kayla.

"Well," Amy added, "I wish for a million bucks."

"I hope your wish doesn't come true," said Kayla.

"Why?"

"Because then we'll be surrounded by a million male deer. They're bucks, get it?"

"That was bad," Amy groaned. "Okay, I wish we had a bag full of money."

The girls were somewhat cranky the next morning because they didn't have much room to sleep in the cramped, stuffy van. With the windows open, the trio made easy targets for hungry mosquitoes.

"I have to be at work in thirty minutes," said Jan. "You two stay here and stick together. Amy, you listen to your sister. And, Kayla, don't act bossy. I'll be back at two o'clock. If there are any leftovers at the café, I'll bring them home. If you get hungry before then"—she reached in her purse and pulled out three dollars—"here's some money. That's all we can afford. But don't worry. Someday soon, we'll have plenty of money."

After Jan hugged her daughters and drove off, the girls ambled over to the campground's general store and watched people come and go. Next, they visited the stables to look at the horses. As the summer sun rose higher in the sky, they played at Slick Rock Falls. But they soon tired of that and decided to hike Clay Creek Trail. The girls walked through a forest of hardwoods, hemlock, and rhododendron, rock-hopping several times over twisting Clay Creek.

While fording the stream at one point where the water was a few feet deep, Kayla gingerly stepped from one rock to another. When she reached the other side, she warned Amy, "Be careful. The moss makes some of the rocks slippery."

"No problem." Amy began carefully walking across. But she'd made it only about halfway when she slipped, lost her balance, and tumbled into the water.

"Aaahhh!" she screamed, as she scrambled to her feet, soaked from the waist down. Kayla, who was laughing so hard that tears rolled down her face, offered her hand.

"Nice splash," roared Kayla. "I give it a nine point five."

Amy then grabbed Kayla's hand. But instead of trying to climb up the bank, she gave a yank. Unprepared for her sister's jerk, Kayla lost her balance and toppled into the creek.

"Ha-ha!" said Amy. "I give you a nine point two. I win."

Half in jest and half in anger, Kayla slapped the water so it splashed in Amy's face. Amy retaliated by scooping up a handful of water and flinging it at Kayla. Within seconds the two were completely drenched, along with their towels, which had drifted downstream.

The girls waded downstream to retrieve their towels. Then Amy noticed a zippered pouch about twelve inches long and six inches wide, stuck between two rocks a few inches below the surface.

"Hey. What's this?" Amy wondered as she picked it up. The girls climbed onto a sun-kissed boulder in the middle of the stream. Amy placed the bag on her lap, unzipped it, peeked inside, and gasped.

"Well, what's in it?" asked Kayla.

Amy, her eyes wide with astonishment, whispered, "Money! Lots of money!"

"Yeah, right. Let me see." Amy handed over the bag. Kayla opened it and pulled out several hundred-dollar bills. "Oh, geez! It *is* money!" She quickly closed the pouch and wrapped it in her wet towel. "Let's get out of here!"

The two scampered back to the trail, then veered off the path to a secluded spot among a stand of trees. "No one will see us in here," whispered Kayla. She unzipped the bag again and dumped out twenties, fifties, and hundred-dollar bills. "Look at this! I've never seen so much money in my life!"

"Let's see how much is there," urged Amy. The two began counting the wet bills. The money added up to $4,820.

"Where do you suppose it came from?" Amy asked.

"I don't know. There's no name inside. The bag says 'Systemony' on the outside."

"Maybe it was stolen."

"Maybe it was lost," offered Kayla.

"If there's no name, then it's finders, keepers; losers, weepers, right?"

"It's not our money."

"But we need it," Amy argued. "With this money, we can live in a nice apartment like normal people. It's our money now. We were meant to find it."

"We couldn't keep it even if we wanted to. Mom would make us take it back."

"To whom? There's no name in there. It could be anybody's. Kayla, if there was ever a family who needed this money, it's us."

"Mom will make us turn it over to the police."

Amy raised her eyebrows. "But what if Mom doesn't know about it? What if we keep slipping some money in her purse every day or—"

"Amy. Stop. We're going to tell her."

"Okay, okay," Amy grumbled.

They carefully put the money back into the bag, covered it with a towel, and carried it to their campsite. As soon as Jan arrived home from work, the girls jumped into the van and made her roll up the windows. Then they showed her the money and explained how they found it.

"Let's report this to the park ranger's office immediately," Jan decided without hesitation.

"But, Mom," Amy pleaded. "We need the money."

"It's not ours to keep. Amy, if you had that kind of money and lost it, wouldn't you want someone to do the right thing and return it?"

"I guess so," she replied with a pout.

Jan slid the bag under the seat of the van. Then she walked to the ranger's office. "Did anyone report losing a blue, zippered bank bag with money in it?" she asked.

The ranger looked at his log sheet and shook his head.

"Well, my daughters found a bag in a creek near Slick Rock Falls," Jan explained. "If anyone reports a lost money bag, send that person to Campsite Twenty-Three."

Later that afternoon, Jan and the girls visited Rocky, but they didn't tell him about the money—although Amy was about to burst from keeping the secret. On the way back to the campsite, Amy asked her mother, "If no one claims the money by the end of the day, is it ours?"

"No, honey. We'll check with the sheriff's office and state

police. We will not spend a dime of someone else's money, no matter how badly we need it. It could be ours if nobody claims it after a few weeks or months."

"Oh, I hope no one claims it," said Amy, crossing her fingers. "Admit it, Mom, you hope so, too, right?"

"It's very tempting to say that. But if it's money from a crime, we would be spending dirty money. If it's honest money that was lost, then the rightful owner should come forward and claim it."

The family had just finished dinner when a middle-aged, bearded man entered their campsite. "Pardon me," he said to Jan. "My name is George Hanson. The park ranger said you found a blue-zippered bank bag."

"My daughters did. Can you describe what it says on the outside of the bag?"

"'Systemony.'"

The girls' hearts sank. "There goes our new apartment and new clothes," Amy whimpered to Kayla.

"How much money was in it?" Jan asked George.

"Exactly four thousand eight hundred twenty dollars."

"What kind of bills?"

"Twenties, fifties, and hundreds," he answered. "Please, if you have it, I need it back because it's not mine. It belongs to the company I work for. I was supposed to deposit it at the bank. I figured that since it was Saturday, it wouldn't matter when I made the deposit, as long as it was sometime over the weekend. I took my family to the park here with plans to deposit the money later. I didn't want to leave the money in the car, so I carried it with me in my backpack while the kids went swimming at Slick Rock Falls. Then we took a little hike, and I fell crossing a stream. I didn't realize that my backpack was open and the bank bag fell out. I discovered the loss when I went to the bank. I didn't think there was a chance that anyone would find the money, much less report it."

"Wait here," Jan told him. "I'll get your money."

While her mother retrieved the bag, Amy walked over to the picnic table and began to cry. "It's not fair. We need it more than a big company does."

Jan returned with the bag and told George, "Count it. You'll find that it's all there."

After counting the money, the man broke out in a big grin. "I can't tell you how happy I am. First of all, you saved my job. Second, I'd have been forced to pay the money back. And third, it's nice to know that you and your girls are such honest folks."

Amy stopped crying and walked over to George. "There wouldn't be a reward for finding this, would there?"

"Amy Elaine Templeton!" Jan scolded her. "Shame on you. You don't need a reward for doing what's right. Remember the saying, 'Virtue is its own reward.'"

George rubbed his chin and shuffled his feet. "I'm in a dilemma. The company would surely give you a reward if it knew what happened. But if I tell them what happened, I'll lose my job. I only have twenty dollars on me, which you're welcome to have. I know it's not much, but—"

"Keep your twenty," said Jan.

"Mom, please," Amy begged.

George pulled out a billfold from his back pocket. "It's plain to see how decent and honest you are. Allow me to give the girls two ten-dollar bills. It's not a reward. It's a gift from me to them, a token of my appreciation. And here are four lottery tickets.

Who knows, maybe you'll get lucky. The big drawing is tonight."

With both girls pleading, Jan reluctantly let them accept the twenty dollars and the lottery tickets.

"Wow!" exclaimed Amy, fingering her ten-dollar bill. "We could splurge and get a pizza and ice cream or—"

"Save it for something worthwhile," Jan suggested. "It's your decision. You each get ten dollars to spend on whatever you want."

That night, after dinner, the girls stretched out on the picnic table and looked up at the stars again.

"Mom," said Amy, "I'm sorry if I acted like a greedy pig before. Seeing all that money made me go crazy. Here, I want you to have my ten dollars. Use it for groceries or gas."

"Me too, Mom," said Kayla. "Here."

"Girls, you are the greatest," said Jan, hugging them. "But you keep your money. I swear, somehow we'll see better days."

The next morning was Jan's day off from work. She walked over to the park store and bought the Sunday paper. When she returned to the campsite, she began scanning the want ads, hoping to find a better job.

Amy looked sleepily at the front page. When she saw the words WINNING LOTTERY NUMBERS, she perked up. "Oh, I forgot about our lottery tickets!" she said. She ran back into the van and grabbed the tickets.

"Don't get your hopes up," warned Jan. "The odds are against anyone winning."

The numbers on the first three lottery tickets failed to match the winning numbers in the paper. Then Amy compared the fourth one. Nine on the ticket, nine in the paper . . . eighteen on the ticket, eighteen in the paper . . . twenty-eight on the ticket, twenty-eight in the paper.

By now, Amy's heart was beating so hard she could feel her head pounding. *Oh, please, please, please,* she thought. Twelve on the ticket, twelve in the paper. *One more and we'll be rich, rich, rich! All our troubles will be over! After all our bad luck, maybe it's our turn for a big break.*

Amy broke out in a sweat and her body began to shake. Thirty-two on the ticket and . . . Her heart sank and her body went limp. Thirty-nine in the paper.

Amy burst into tears. "Oh, Mom, we missed by only one number! We would've been millionaires! But we're still just homeless people. Life is so unfair. We came so close and we get nothing, nothing, nothing. When will it get better? When?"

Jan scurried to the other side of the table. "Amy, did you say we got all but one number?"

"Yes, we just missed winning. It would hurt less to not have any of the numbers than to come that close and lose." Amy gathered the tickets and was about to rip them up, but Jan grabbed her hand and stopped her.

Jan compared the last ticket with the numbers in the paper. She let out a joyful yell. "We didn't win the big jackpot, but we're still winners!"

Amy asked, "What do you mean?"

"Look, it's right here in the paper! 'Four out of five correct numbers pays four thousand eight hundred twenty dollars!'"

"Four thousand eight hundred twenty dollars?" cried Amy. "That's the exact total of the money we found yesterday!"

"See, I told you things would get better," said her gleeful mother. "I just didn't expect it would come in the form of the greatest coincidence of our lives."

The Flight to Serendipity

Jensen Beach, Florida, May 20, 1976: Eight sweaty, sand-covered young men lined up against each other, four on a side, while the white-capped waves of the Atlantic Ocean slapped against the shore.

"Hut one! Hut two! Hike!" shouted Bill Santo. When the football snapped into his hands, he drifted back and scanned the beach. He saw receiver Ken Blake fake right and then sprint left toward the water, leaving his defender scrambling five feet behind him. Bill fired a bullet, but the sea breeze slowed the ball just enough for the defender to catch up to Ken. He leaped high to make a fingertip reception and then tucked the ball to his belly as his body splashed into the shallow water.

Ken came up sputtering but held the ball in the air. "Touchdown!" he yelled triumphantly. "We win!"

His teammates whooped victoriously and then pounded on Ken, playfully shoving him under the water. The four of them wrestled in the surf before coming out and shaking hands with their opponents.

The eight young men had just graduated from Augustana College and were in Florida for a final weeklong fling before heading out into the real world.

As they toweled off, Ken suddenly looked at his hand. "Oh, no!" he groaned. "My class ring is missing!"

"We just got our rings two weeks ago," said Bill. "Don't tell me you lost yours already!"

"Come on, help me find it."

For the next hour, the young men scoured the beach where they had been playing touch football, but it was a fruitless search. Ken's two-hundred-dollar gold and topaz ring was apparently lost forever.

"It probably got washed out in the ocean," said Bill.

"Maybe it'll wash in one day," said Ken. "I hope whoever finds it will try to return it. My name and the school are engraved on it."

Jensen Beach, Florida, March 8, 1978: The early-morning sun peeked over the calm ocean, casting an orange glow on the faces of eighteen-year-old Terri Manchester and her mother, Pat. Armed with pails, they ambled along the beach, their eyes scanning for shells that had been driven ashore by an overnight storm. "The shelling is pretty good today," said Pat.

"Yeah, I wish it were this easy getting a man," Terri joked. "I haven't been doing too well in the dating game."

"The right one will come along. You'll see."

"Ooh, a sand dollar," said Terri. She reached down and picked it up. As she did, she noticed a sliver of gold buried in the wet sand. She poked around with her fingers and then exclaimed, "Mother, look! A ring!"

She cleaned it off in the water and then examined it closely. "It's a school ring, class of seventy-six, Augustana College. Do you know where that is?"

"It's a small school in Illinois."

"The ring belongs to someone named Ken Blake. It's a nice topaz. It's probably worth a few hundred dollars."

"Maybe you could call the college and track down this Ken Blake," Pat suggested.

"Sure. Maybe he's tall, dark, and handsome—and single. Maybe he's the man of my dreams."

That afternoon, Terri placed a call to Augustana College in Rock Island, Illinois, but the office had no record of a student named Ken Blake.

"Oh, well, so much for meeting the man of my dreams," she told her mother.

"What are you going to do with the ring, Terri?"

"I don't know. I guess I'll keep it for a while." She tossed it in her jewelry box and forgot all about it.

Stuart, Florida, June 3, 1982: "How is the packing coming along, Terri?" asked Pat, surveying the mess of boxes scattered around her daughter's bedroom.

"Slowly. I didn't realize I had accumulated so much junk growing up. I'm trying to sort what stuff I'll take with me, what to store in the attic, and what to give away. This is the hard part about getting married and moving away."

"No, the hard part is actually saying good-bye and moving away," Pat said tearfully.

"Don't start crying, Mother, or I'll be a weeping machine."

As she sorted her jewelry, Terri picked up Ken Blake's class ring and said, "I don't know why I held on to this. It's not doing anyone any good in my jewelry box." She tossed the ring into one of several boxes marked for the charity gift shop. "I guess it should go for a good cause."

Orlando, Florida, June 5, 1982: As Terri and her husband, Jack, unpacked in their first apartment, she opened a small box and was surprised to see Ken Blake's class ring. "The things in this box were supposed to go to the thrift shop, Jack," she said.

"Sorry, honey. My mistake."

"Oh, well, I guess I'll keep them for a while." She tossed the ring into one of her two jewelry boxes.

Clermont, Florida, October 15, 1989: "Jack, do you hear something in our bedroom?" asked Terri. She was sitting next to her husband on the living-room couch, watching the eleven o'clock news.

Jack used the remote control to turn down the sound on the television set. "I don't hear anything. We've only been in this new house a few weeks. Maybe you aren't used to all the sounds it makes."

"No, this was different, like a thud," Terri insisted. "I'll go check on David first." Even though her five-year-old son slept in a bedroom on the other side of the house, she made sure he was safe before she investigated.

As Terri crossed the living room, she heard another sound, like a tinkling. "Jack, will you come with me? I think there's someone in our bedroom!" she whispered anxiously.

Jack shook his head. "Nah. You're hearing things." He turned his attention back to the TV set.

"Thanks a lot," she muttered angrily. Terri tiptoed down the hall. In one motion she opened the door and flipped on the light switch. She stood in shock. A man in a ski mask was holding her two jewelry boxes, scooping up rings and bracelets that had spilled out of one of the boxes. He turned and glared at her. Then he grabbed a handful of the fallen jewelry off the floor and leaped out the open ground-floor window.

Recovering from her fear-stricken daze, Terri screamed, bringing Jack into the room. "There was a robber in our bedroom!" she shouted. "I told you I heard something! You never listen to me. Now look what happened." She opened the drawer to the chest where she had hidden her jewelry boxes under her sweaters. "He took all my jewelry!"

"Not quite everything," said Jack, holding up Ken Blake's class ring. "The thief must have dropped this when he slipped out the window."

Terri grabbed the ring and hurled it against the wall. The ring ricocheted and hit the bedside table before disappearing behind their platform waterbed.

Clermont, Florida, July 27, 1992: When Pat walked into Terri's bedroom, Terri said, "I've drained the waterbed, so now we can dismantle the wood frame and platform and junk them."

"But I thought you liked the waterbed."

Terri shook her head. "Now that Jack is out of my life, I want to get rid of it. I never liked it much anyway."

"How is David handling the divorce?"

"Pretty good for an eight-year-old. He still sees his dad twice a week, and he doesn't feel like he's caught in the middle because it wasn't one of those bitter split-ups. I think he's glad that you came to visit. You know how much he adores his grandma."

When they hauled out the dismantled bed, Terri noticed a gold object tucked in a spot where the carpet met the baseboard. She bent down, picked it up, and smiled. "Do you remember this, Mother?"

"It looks like a man's ring."

"It's the ring that won't go away. Remember, I found a class ring at the beach years ago?"

"Yes. I thought that after you couldn't find the owner you gave it away to charity."

"I tried to. But for a variety of reasons, it stayed with me. When we were robbed, the burglar took everything but this ring. I found it and was so angry about the burglary and with Jack that I threw the ring across the room. It ended up rolling behind the waterbed, out of my reach. I forgot all about it until now."

"What are you going to do with it?"

"I'm going to keep it. There must be a reason why it simply won't leave my possession."

Airspace over Gainesville, Florida, March 18, 1996: "This is so awesome, Dad!" declared Seth Blake. The twelve-year-old boy leaned over the side of the rattan basket that dangled under a red-and-yellow hot-air balloon. He gazed down at the patchwork shades of green farmland and the pale blue springs and ponds two thousand feet below. "Thanks for taking me. This is way cool!"

"I can't think of anybody I'd rather have along as my first passenger," declared Ken Blake.

For Ken, ballooning was love at first flight. He got hooked on the sport in 1994, following his divorce from Caryn, whom he had married after graduating from Augustana College. They had lived in Des Moines, Iowa, where Ken took a job in banking. Although his career improved, his marriage did not. While Caryn and Seth remained in Des Moines after the divorce, Ken moved to Gainesville to take a new position as president of a bank in 1993.

A friend of his introduced him to ballooning. After nearly a year of riding with friends, Ken got his license but didn't take any passengers up for a while. He was waiting until Seth could visit him on spring break. Ken wanted his son to be his first passenger.

"It's magical," Seth marveled. "I feel like I'm in the movie *The Wizard of Oz*."

"Now you know how I feel," said Ken.

"There's no wind in my face. How come?"

"Because you're floating with the wind."

Since the first hot-air balloon was launched in France in 1783, the basics of flying one have remained unchanged: To go up, heated air is pumped into the balloon; to go down, the hot air is released through a vent at the top of the balloon. As for direction, the pilot is strictly at the mercy of the winds.

Ken opened the valve on the burner, which was mounted above the passenger seat. It sent a loud blast of propane-fueled flames shooting up into the mouth of the envelope—the colorful, strong fabric that holds the hot air. Within a minute, the balloon had climbed another thousand feet.

"How come we don't carry parachutes?" asked Seth.

"If the burner goes out and for some reason can't be

reignited, the balloon itself acts as a parachute," his father explained.

"What happens if a bird flies into the side of the balloon?"

"It would likely bounce off. The envelope fabric is much tougher than it might look. Boy, you're full of questions today. Got any more?"

"Are you dating anyone?"

"Whoa! That came from left field. No, son. I've been too busy with work during the week and ballooning on weekends. Anyway, I'm not really looking to date yet. What about you? Are you dating?"

"Dad, please. I'm too young."

The balloon floated silently and effortlessly through central Florida. About an hour into the flight, Ken looked over the side. "Hmmm, we're picking up speed. I don't see our chase crew."

The chase crew consisted of three friends in a van who were following the balloon so that when it landed, they could retrieve and deflate it and pick up the passengers.

Ken looked behind him and made a face. "Darn, when did those clouds show up? It looks like a storm is coming in. We'd better start looking for a place to land."

He vented hot air out of the crown at the top, and the balloon began to descend. But it hit a pocket of warm air known as a thermal and began climbing again. A gust whipped the balloon to the southeast.

"It's best we get this baby down as quickly as we can," said Ken, venting even more hot air out of the balloon. The craft began drifting down, but gusts had shoved it away from the open fields and farmland, and into a residential area. Ken didn't want to alarm his son, but he was concerned that under these breezy conditions, the balloon could plow into a house, a tree, or—even more dangerous—power lines.

The balloon was about five hundred feet off the ground when they reached calmer air, much to Ken's relief. Although he still couldn't steer the craft, he wanted to land it before he risked ramming into an obstruction.

"The bad news is we're in a residential area," he told Seth. "The good news is that the lots here are quite large."

At two hundred feet, Ken spotted a petite, brown-haired woman washing her car in the driveway in front of her house. "Hello! Hello!" he yelled from his basket. The woman looked to her left and right but didn't see anyone. "Look up! Look up!" Ken shouted.

She did and let out a shriek of surprise. "Oh, my goodness!"

"Do you mind if we land in your backyard?"

"Well, uh . . . no! Be my guest."

Ken waved to her and then pulled on the cord to vent out more hot air. "Keep your knees bent and relaxed," he told Seth. Seconds later, the basket hit the soft earth, bounced a couple of times, and then came to rest as the deflated envelope slowly sagged to the ground.

"Hey, we made it, son!"

"All right, Dad!" said Seth, giving his father a high-five. "What an awesome trip!"

The woman, now accompanied by several excited neighbors, hurried over to the balloon. After Ken enlisted their help to secure the lines and squeeze the hot air from the envelope, his chase crew arrived to finish the job.

Ken then sought out the owner of the property. He was pleasantly surprised at how attractive she looked in her baseball cap, jeans, and sweatshirt. "Thanks for letting me land here," he said, shaking her hand.

"It's not every day that a hot-air balloon lands in my backyard," she remarked. "Welcome to my little bit of heaven. My name is Terri Manchester-Carter."

"Hi, I'm Ken Blake. My son, Seth, is over there helping the chase crew." Noticing a look of astonishment on her face, he said, "Is something the matter?"

"You're Ken Blake?"

"I was the last time I checked. Why?"

"Did you go to Augustana College?"

"Yeah."

"Did you graduate in 1976?"

"Yes. Why?"

"You came to the right spot, Ken Blake, because I have a surprise for you. I'll be right back."

Terri ran into the house and quickly returned. She held out her closed hand and then opened it. "Ta-da!" she yelled, displaying the gold and topaz ring in her palm.

Ken picked it up and exclaimed, "My ring!"

"What are the odds of your landing in the backyard of the very person who found your ring?" she asked in wonder.

"But . . . but how did you get it?" Ken stammered.

"I found it on Jensen Beach one day in 1978. I called Augustana College in Illinois, but they didn't have a record of any student named Ken Blake."

"That's because I went to Augustana College in Sioux Falls, South Dakota," Ken explained.

"I can't tell you how many times I tried to get rid of this ring, but it always found a way to stay with me," said Terri. "Finally, I decided to keep it. I knew there had to be a reason. I just didn't know what it would be—until now."

"I can't tell you how grateful I am that you kept it for all these years." *She is really pretty*, Ken thought.

"I can't tell you how amazed I am that you landed in my backyard to reclaim it." *Wow, this guy is gorgeous*, Terri told herself.

"It must be serendipity."

Clermont, Florida, August 1, 1997: The minister turned to Terri and said, "Do you, Terri, take Ken to be your lawfully wedded husband, to have and to hold, in sickness and in health, for richer or poorer, for better or worse, for as long as you both shall live?"

"I do."

"Do you, Ken, take Terri to be your lawfully wedded wife, to have and to hold, in sickness and in health, for richer or poorer, for better or worse, for as long as you both shall live?"

"I do."

"Then, by the powers vested in me by the great state of Florida, I do hereby pronounce you two husband and wife."

Too True Stories

The giant boa constrictor wrapped its thick body around Kelsie. Its grip grew tighter and tighter. The reptile turned its sinister head toward its victim and almost seemed to mock the helpless teenage girl. Its green eyes stared at Kelsie with an evil twinkle, as if it took great joy in squeezing the life out of her.

Kelsie was indeed helpless. She couldn't even scream. When she tried, only a weak, frightened squeak came out of her mouth as the last few gasps of air were forced from her lungs by the merciless snake.

What a way to die, Kelsie thought, closing her eyes for the last time.

"Hey, Mom!" shouted Wyatt Hagerman, bounding into the kitchen. "I got an A on my writing assignment and . . ." The fourteen-year-old boy stopped in mid-sentence when he saw a worried look on his mother's face. "Something's wrong, isn't it?"

"Your sister had a very frightening experience today. We just got back from the hospital."

"What happened?"

"Kelsie was with her class at the science museum. They were in the reptile room, and—well, you know how bold your sister is. They asked for a volunteer, and she naturally stepped forward. Then they took this big boa constrictor out of its cage and let her hold it."

"It was the scariest day of my life," declared his sixteen-year-old sister, as she walked into the room.

"Are you okay?" Wyatt asked.

"Yeah, I am now. But this morning I thought I was going to die. The snake curator put the boa over my shoulders, and I held it with no problem, even though it was heavy and moving around more than I would've liked. Then Chiara—you know, Little Miss Priss—screamed and fainted. That freaked the snake, and it began wrapping its whole body around me. Meanwhile, the curator went to help Chiara, because she hit her head on the edge of the table and was bleeding. So now everyone was freaking out—including me.

"The boa squeezed me harder and harder. I tried to pry it off, but every time I got one section loose, the rest of it squeezed tighter. I yelled at the curator for help, but he couldn't get the snake off me. I was really scared, because I could hardly breathe. The curator shouted for help, and Ted and Mickey came over. The three of them finally pulled the snake off me, but by then the boa had squeezed me so tight that I fainted.

"They took me and Chiara to the hospital. I was okay, just a little sore around the ribs. Chiara needed five stitches in her head.

"The curator was very upset. He said the boa had never behaved like that before. Apparently, they always make sure the snake is fed before it's handled, because the food makes it sluggish. The curator assumed the snake had been fed but it hadn't, so it was hungry. Then, when Chiara screamed and everyone shouted, the snake became agitated and began squeezing me."

Wyatt leaned against the kitchen wall and shook his head. "This is unbelievable!" he exclaimed. "Look at me. I'm trembling all over."

"Gee, I didn't think you cared that much," Kelsie said.

"No, I'm not talking about you," Wyatt said. He handed his sister the paper he had been holding and said, "Look at this. It's a story I wrote for English class last week. I got an A on it."

She glanced at the title: "'Squeeze.' So?"

"Go ahead and read it, Kelsie."

Kelsie Hagerman walked through the dense jungle, a feeling of doom lurking in the pit of her stomach. Suddenly, what she thought was a branch began to move, and a pair of evil green eyes glared at her. Kelsie screamed in terror. But it was too late. The giant boa constrictor dropped on her, wrapping her in its deadly coils.

Kelsie glared at Wyatt and said, "What is this? Some sort of sick joke?"

"No, that's what's so incredible," he said. "I wrote that last week. It's all about how you were attacked by a boa constrictor. And now—days later—you actually do get attacked by a boa."

"You really are sick," Kelsie snapped, flinging the story at him. "I nearly get killed, and you come up with this twisted joke."

"I swear to you that I wrote it last week. If you don't

53

believe me, just ask Miss Conwell. She's the one who read it and gave me an A. It's the weirdest coincidence I've ever experienced."

"Wyatt, are you saying you're psychic?"

"No. I've never made a prediction that's come true—except the one about you and Rick breaking up within a month."

"Don't remind me," she said with a shudder. Staring at her brother, she warned, "I definitely plan on asking Miss Conwell about this. And if you're making fun of my near-death experience, I'll make sure you have one yourself."

"All right, kids, that's enough," ordered their mother. "You know better than to make threats, Kelsie. And, Wyatt, you wouldn't really be that insensitive, would you?"

"Of course not. I'm telling you the truth."

The next day, with Wyatt by her side, Kelsie asked Miss Conwell about his story. "Isn't it uncanny?" the teacher said in bewilderment. "Wyatt wrote it last week, and it pretty much came true—except the part about the jungle and the fact that you died."

"See?" Wyatt told Kelsie. "It's just a coincidence."

"Well, from now on, leave me out of your stories, okay?"

Wyatt agreed. However, he couldn't resist using the names of his friends in future stories to see if what he wrote came true for them. It never did, which squelched any hope that he might be psychic.

A year later, for an advanced creative writing course, Wyatt was supposed to write a period piece from the nineteenth century. He composed a tale about a runaway stagecoach carrying a group of screaming passengers. For no particular reason, he named the heroine Kelsie.

Careening down the trail without its driver, the swaying, rocking stagecoach was headed straight into tragedy. The terrified screams of the passengers couldn't drown out the sounds of the wooden wheels crashing against the rocks and the thundering hooves of the out-of-control team of horses.

"I'm not ready to die!" Kelsie yelled to the others. With all her might, she climbed out through the window and up onto the roof. Then she crawled to the driver's seat and grabbed the reins. "Whoa!" she yelled. "Whoa!" But the horses paid her no attention.

She yanked on the reins as hard as she could, but it was no use. Now she had another problem. A sturdy oak tree stood straight in the path of the runaway stagecoach. Kelsie tried to turn the horses away, but each lead horse wanted to go its separate way. One leaned to the left, the other to the right. The yoke between the horses slammed against the tree. The stagecoach split right in half, spilling everyone to the ground.

About a week after he wrote it, Wyatt brought the paper home to show his mother, who always read and enjoyed everything he wrote. "Got another A," Wyatt announced, waving the paper in his hand.

His mother, who was on the phone, looked up, smiled, and mouthed, "Congratulations" before returning to her phone conversation. When she finished, she told Wyatt, "That was Kelsie. She's having a great time in Colorado with her church group. They were rock climbing yesterday and went hiking this morning."

"What a lucky stiff. She got to start her spring break three days early."

"So, you received another A, huh?"

"Yeah, it's a pretty good story. Lots of blood and guts and bodies flying all over."

"Sounds gross. Let me read it."

As he munched on a granola bar, Wyatt noticed his mother was frowning. When she finished reading his story, she looked down and nervously rubbed her temples.

"You didn't like it?" he asked her.

"It was well-written, Wyatt. But did you have to put Kelsie's name in it?"

"What's the big deal? I made her the heroine. Hey, you're not thinking about what happened with the snake story last year, are you? Come on, Mom. That was a fluke. Besides, Kelsie's not riding in a stagecoach."

"No, but she told me they were going to be riding in a horse-drawn wagon in the mountains later today."

"Oh, you don't think—"

"I just have an uneasy feeling. I know this sounds silly, and I know her snake attack and your snake story were just a coincidence, but why take any chances? I'm going to tell her not to go."

"Mom, you're being silly."

"I'd rather be a fool than sit idly by and let my only daughter get hurt. Now where is that phone number?"

Mrs. Hagerman dialed the inn where the church group was staying. "Hello, may I speak to Kelsie Hagerman, please? Oh, they did? Is there any way to reach them? I see. Yes, please have her call home the moment she returns. Thank you." Turning to Wyatt, she said, "It's too late. They already left on their ride."

"Mom, nothing is going to happen," Wyatt claimed.

"You're being paranoid over nothing. I've written dozens of stories with names of people I know, and none of them ever came true."

"I suppose you're right. What can I say? I'm a mother, so I'm supposed to worry. It's part of my job description."

Hours later, long after the dinner dishes had been washed and put away, the Hagermans still had not heard from Kelsie. Seeing his mother fret, Wyatt tried to calm her. "She's fine, Mom. They probably forgot to give her the message, or maybe it was—"

The ringing of the phone interrupted him. In a flash, his mother pounced on the receiver. "Hello? Is that you, Kelsie?"

"Mom," said Kelsie in a shaky voice on the verge of tears. "First, I want to tell you that I'm all right."

"Oh, my gosh! What happened? You got in an accident on the wagon, right?"

"Yes, Mom. How did you know?"

"The horses bolted, you had no driver, and the wagon split in two!"

"Who told you?"

"Wyatt."

"Wyatt? How did he find out?"

"Never mind, Kelsie. Tell me what happened. Are you hurt?"

"Bruised, but otherwise okay. We're all fine, just shaken up. We went on this nice horse-drawn wagon ride on an old dirt trail. It was really pretty going through the woods and everything. After we stopped for a break, we were climbing back into the wagon when suddenly the two horses got spooked by a low-flying military jet. They lurched forward just as the driver was getting on. He was thrown to the ground, and the horses took off with all eight of us girls in the wagon. Before we knew it, we were moving at a full gallop.

"The driver was running like mad after the wagon, but there was no way he could catch it. By now all of us were screaming, because the horses were galloping at what seemed like the speed of light. No one was doing anything, so I climbed over everybody and reached up to the driver's seat and pulled back on a large wooden lever that I assumed was the brake. I pulled on it so hard that it started to smoke, but it didn't slow the wagon down enough.

"I was holding on for dear life, while some of the girls were threatening to jump. I yelled at them not to. But then I saw that we were nearing a cliff, and I knew we had to jump or we'd all die. Just then the horses saw the cliff, and they made a ninety-degree turn. The wagon leaned on two wheels. I thought for sure we'd roll over, but we didn't. We turned off the road and were bouncing through a mountain meadow. I was screaming at the horses and the girls were screaming at me, because we were aiming for a telephone pole.

"The horses were hooked together by a large wooden yoke. One horse went to the left of the pole, and the other to the right. There was a tremendous impact when the yoke hit the pole. The yoke broke, freeing the horses, and everyone but me flew out of the wagon, which literally split in two. The girls lay all over the place like rag dolls. It was a miracle no one was seriously hurt."

"Oh, thank goodness you're all right," her mother sighed.

"Yeah. So who told Wyatt about the accident?"

"No one, Kelsie. He wrote about a runaway stagecoach and

how a woman named Kelsie climbed out onto the roof and tried to rein in the horses, but the coach split in two when it hit a tree, spilling everyone."

"Wait a minute. Wyatt wrote about me?"

"Yes, he used your name as the heroine in the story."

"He used my name last year with the snake! Now he did it again! What's he trying to do, kill me with his writing?"

Wyatt got on the phone. "Kelsie, I'm really sorry. It was just another coincidence. I've written dozens of stories using the names of friends and relatives, and nothing ever came true."

"Promise me you will never, ever use my name in anything else you write."

"I promise. In fact, I won't use the name of anyone I know, even if it's a sweet story where nobody gets hurt."

For the rest of the year, Wyatt stuck by his word—with one exception. He wrote a first-person love story about a boy who fell for a girl named Marcy. In real life, Marcy happened to be the name of a girl Wyatt wanted to date. But this time life didn't imitate art. When Wyatt asked Marcy for a date, she turned him down flat.

Waiting for Destiny

The basketball game was turning ugly.

The Riverview High Raiders and the Lido High Panthers kept bumping, nudging, and hacking each other so much the refs' cheeks hurt from constantly blowing their whistles.

Lido's sophomore star, Marcus Fain, set the tone with his aggressive defense. He shadowed every move of Riverview's Cordell Jenkins. The two were friends, but in this game they trash-talked as they ran up and down the court and traded several hard fouls.

Early in the fourth quarter, Coach Bart Djedowicz called time and scolded Marcus. "We can't afford to have you foul out. Get in Jenkins's face but don't mug him."

"Don't mug him? He ought to be tackled," Marcus countered. "Have you seen what he's been doing to me? He's grabbing and scratching and jabbing me—and those refs are blind. He's been dissing me the whole game. If he doesn't watch out, he's gonna get a forearm to that big mouth of his."

Marcus's eyes blazed with a loathing that the young coach

had never seen before in the normally mild-mannered teen. It wasn't like Marcus to talk like that. The fifteen-year-old was bright, had a good sense of humor, and came from a home where his parents, Bob and Helene, taught him respect for education and other people. But over the past two weeks, Bart had noticed a change in Marcus's attitude. He seemed more edgy, and not as witty as he usually was. On the court, Marcus's scoring had slipped from an average of fourteen points a game down to eight. Worse, his defense had lapsed badly.

"Marcus, stay in control," Bart told him. "You've got only one foul left. We need you. Play smart, play wise. We're only down by five, so we have plenty of time to catch them."

But Riverview pulled away late in the game. When it was obvious Lido was going to lose, Cordell fouled Marcus hard enough to send the Lido High star sprawling into the seats behind the basket. The two glared at each other as Marcus stepped to the line and then sank both meaningless shots. Rather than run upcourt, Marcus stayed at the free-throw line. As Cordell inbounded the ball and started upcourt, he ran past Marcus, who stuck out his elbow at nose-level and slammed it into Cordell's face.

Cordell staggered backward and tumbled to the floor, clutching his bleeding nose. Then, in a rage, he charged after Marcus, grabbed him from behind, and threw him to the floor. The two began punching each other, triggering a melee as players from both teams converged at center court. Coaches, officials, fans, and police joined the fray, trying to yank players off one another.

Bart battled his way into the fight and found Marcus flailing away on top of Cordell. The glare in Marcus's eyes made Bart think of an angry wild animal attacking its prey. "Marcus! Stop! No, Marcus!" Bart bent over, trying to shove Marcus off Cordell. Just then another player plowed into Bart, causing him to lose his balance. His left leg was pinned between two squirming bodies, and when Bart fell, he twisted his knee. The coach cried out in pain. For a moment, he forgot about Marcus. He just wanted to get himself untangled from this wild mass of raging humanity.

Five minutes later, after everyone had been pulled apart, Bart grabbed Marcus by the arm and limped with him over to the bench. "Have you gone stark raving mad?" Bart bellowed. "That forearm shiver was a cheap shot. Look what you caused!"

"I don't care," snapped Marcus. "I'm through taking guff from anyone."

One of the refs came over and brusquely told Bart, "We've declared this game over. Too much bad blood."

"Yeah, and I've got some of it on my new tie," the gangly coach said. "Maybe I should stick to teaching English."

Marcus, who was walking away, muttered, "Yeah, maybe you should, Coach Brillo."

The coach had been tagged with the nickname because of his thick, wiry black hair. But no player had ever dared called him that to his face. If his players had trouble pronouncing his last name, they called him Coach D or Mr. D.

Bart knew that something beyond the game was definitely bothering Marcus. But before he could say anything else, Marcus's mother rushed up to her son. "Marcus, are you hurt?"

He scowled at her. "I'm fine. I was just defending myself."

"It looked more like you were attacking."

"You don't know anything about what happens on the

court," Marcus snapped before storming off.

Bart had never seen Marcus behave that way, especially toward his mother. "I think he's upset and a little embarrassed over—"

Helene interrupted the coach with a wave of her hand. "Don't defend him. He knows he did wrong. He's made several bad choices lately."

"Do you know why?"

"My husband, Bob, and I separated a few weeks ago," she said barely above a whisper. "He's got this screwy idea that he's going to strike it rich by investing in a diamond mine in Botswana, in Africa. He's going over there next week. It's really affected Marcus. My son won't talk to me about his feelings, but he's hurting inside. Maybe you can reach him."

"Let me see if I can talk to him. Trust me, I know what he's going through."

Later, after Marcus had cooled down and taken his shower, Bart asked him, "Mind if I drive you home?"

Marcus eyed him warily and shrugged. "Sorry about the game, Coach," he mumbled. "I screwed up and lost my head."

"Yeah, you did. You'll probably be suspended from the team. You're responsible for your actions, and when your actions are wrong, you pay the price."

Marcus didn't say a word, just gave a half-hearted nod.

When they got into the car, Bart said, "Your mom told me about your dad."

"So? There's nothing you can do about it."

"I can try to help you deal with your pain."

"What do you know about pain?"

"Well, for starters . . ." Bart pointed to his knee. That brought a faint smile to Marcus's lips. "For another, I still have pain in my heart from when my dad abandoned his family. I was only eight, but I remember everything as if it was yesterday. Dad was a successful architect, a funny, bright, loving father who always had time to take me to a Dodgers or a Lakers game. He was everything you could ask for in a dad.

"Then things went downhill. He'd come home and pick a fight with my mom, often during dinner. I can't tell you how many times she ran into the bedroom and locked the door and cried. Then he'd find some made-up reason to jump down my throat.

"This went on for a year. He lost his job, and soon we lost the house and had to move in with my grandparents. He and my mom separated, and she held down two jobs to support me. My dad just disappeared—no good-byes, no nothing. Someone said he was somewhere in South America. We never heard from him, not for birthdays or graduations. I don't know if he's dead or alive. All I know is he's out of my life."

Marcus grunted softly. "My dad hasn't abandoned us, at least not yet. He's moved out. He claims it's for the good of the family and that when he returns he'll give us all a much better life. I always thought I lived in the perfect family. Most of my friends never really knew their fathers, or else their parents are divorced. I thought my parents were different, because they loved each other and hardly ever fought. I don't know what went wrong. Maybe the pressure of raising kids—"

"Marcus, the breakup of your parents is not your fault. It's between your mom and your dad. When my dad took off, I blamed myself. Maybe I shouldn't have broken his camera.

Maybe I shouldn't have talked back to him. Maybe I shouldn't have accidentally scratched his car. I was sure I was the cause. Of course, I wasn't. He had his own demons to deal with. Unfortunately, we ended up becoming the victims of his personal battle. Like my dad, your dad has his priorities screwed up. Let's hope your parents will work things out."

The next day, Bart made an appointment to see the doctor because his knee hurt and was badly swollen. When he arrived at the doctor's office, the receptionist told him, "Dr. Carlson has an emergency and is running behind schedule."

"So what else is new," Bart muttered under his breath. He surveyed the waiting room, where five other patients were sitting. "Are they all ahead of me?" The receptionist nodded. Fortunately, Bart had brought plenty of book reports to grade. He found a seat across from a weathered older man, who was resting his chin on a cane and staring intently at Bart.

Bart gave a half smile and began reading the reports, occasionally glancing at his watch. After nearly an hour of waiting, only he and the older man remained. Bart, now fuming over the delay, wanted to leave, but his knee was really throbbing. *I've invested all this time, I might as well stick it out*, he thought.

He looked across the room at the man and was struck by his strange pose. The man was reading a magazine that he held in his left hand at arm's length. His right arm was cocked with his wrist resting on top of his balding head. *There's only one person I ever knew who read that way*, Bart thought. *I can't believe there are two of them*. He continued to study the man. His glasses were perched near the tip of his pointed nose, and he had a bushy gray-brown mustache that curled up his bony cheeks. His gaunt, pale face looked exceptionally long because of a gray goatee that came to a point at his chin.

Suddenly the man squirmed in his seat and hurriedly tried to reach into his back pocket. "*Ah, ah, eeee, whatchoooo!*" He was about a second too late in getting his handkerchief out before he sneezed. After blowing his nose, he looked up at Bart and murmured, "Excuse me."

That odd sneeze sounded so familiar to Bart that he continued to stare at the man, who gazed right back. Their eyes seemed to be searching for some recognition of the other, like two computer modems trying to link up.

Just then the receptionist entered the room and said, "Mister, um, Dee-jed-o-wish?"

"That's Dee-YED-o-viz," the two patients announced in perfect unison as they rose from their chairs. Once again they stared at each other, this time in complete surprise.

Bart spoke first, spelling out his last name to the man. "D-j-e-d-o-w-i-c-z?"

"That's how I spell it," said the man. "Yosef Djedowicz."

Hearing the complete name stunned Bart so much that he slumped back in his chair. In an almost fearful voice, he looked up and said, "Dad?"

"Bart, is that you?" The man trembled.

Bart nodded. A swirl of emotions—shock, anger, and heartache—raged with hurricane force in his stomach. He didn't know how to react. His father looked so different, so old and worn out. Where was the thick brown hair? Where were the muscular arms? The round, ruddy cheeks? The father he last saw didn't wear glasses, have gray hair, or walk with a cane. His father had left the family at the age of thirty-eight, which meant Yosef was now fifty-eight. Yet this man looked like he was in his seventies.

Leaning on his cane, Yosef tentatively held out his hand toward Bart. But when he saw his son was paralyzed with shock, he withdrew it.

"Yosef?" said the nurse. "The doctor will see you now." Yosef's eyes welled with tears. He turned to Bart and asked, "Your mother, is she all right?"

"She's fine—and happily married."

"And what about you?"

"I teach English and coach basketball at Lido High. I don't have a family."

"I have to see the doctor now, but we have so much to talk about. Please don't leave, Bart."

"Why shouldn't I?" snapped Bart. "You left me and Mom."

"Fate brought you and me here today for a reason. I beg you, Bart, be here when I get out." Then the old man hobbled off with the nurse.

The recollection of all the pain, shame, uncertainty, and hardship that Bart had endured throughout his childhood flooded his brain until he couldn't think straight. He let out a scream and hurled his briefcase across the room, striking a potted plant and toppling it over.

The crash returned Bart to his senses. As he righted the plant and cleaned up the mess, the nurse said, "Bart, we're ready for you now."

Bart shook his head. "No. I've got to get out of here." He headed for the door. But then his father's words, "Fate brought you and me here today for a reason," echoed in his mind. Bart spun around and told the nurse, "Okay, okay. I'll go with you."

After getting the doctor's diagnosis—a severely strained ligament in his knee—Bart returned to the waiting room, where his father was standing.

"Just give me a chance to explain," Yosef pleaded.

"You had twenty years to do that," Bart replied coldly.

"I'm not the same person I was back then," said Yosef. "When I left you, I was a foolish, self-centered man. I needed some space, so I went to Brazil to hunt for gold in the Amazon jungle. I had every intention of returning, but I got involved with some smugglers, was caught, and spent fifteen years in a filthy jail. I got this bum leg down there from a bad infection that was never treated. Now it needs regular medical attention. When I got out of jail, I wandered through South America, too ashamed to come home, too worried that I would bring pain to my family. Eventually, I worked my way back to California. I got my act together, and now I help supervise a food bank down on Clifford Street.

"I can't tell you how many times I wanted to pick up the phone and call. But I had heard that your mother remarried, so I didn't want to butt into her life—or yours. I had screwed up enough.

"Bart, I don't expect you to accept me back in your life right away. But can't we at least take it a step at a time? Let's not lose this opportunity that fate has given us."

Bart took a deep breath and nodded. "Okay. I'll buy you a cup of coffee and we'll talk."

Though they had an awkward and emotional conversation at the café across the street, it brought them close enough to agree to meet again.

"Is this as much of a shock to you as it is to me?" asked

Yosef, as they walked out of the café.

"Probably more so for me," Bart answered. "But it couldn't have come at a better time. Listen, Dad, if you're really serious about trying to have a relationship with me, I need you to do me a favor."

"Anything, son."

"I want you to talk to an acquaintance of mine—the father of one of my players—who's leaving his family to hunt for diamonds in Africa. Sound familiar?"

"Oh, no!" Yosef groaned. "Is he nuts? Let me at him. I guarantee that once he hears my story, he'll rediscover the greatest treasure of his life—his own family."

The next day, Yosef talked to Marcus's father. True to his word, Yosef's guarantee proved as good as gold.

The Lucky Breaks

Fine crystals of snow pelted Jackie Langdon's face as she followed her two older brothers zigzagging down Bearwallow Mountain's intermediate-level ski run. They had taught Jackie well—her form was as smooth and crisp as the Canadian snowpack on this wintry day in 1969. Jackie was on the final run of the family weekend ski trip, which was a gift from her parents for her sixteenth birthday.

When Jackie and her brothers, Sam and Jeff, reached the bottom, they skied to a "slow ski" area and waited for their parents, who were still carefully making their way down the mountain. Jackie lifted her goggles and perched them on her hat to check out one of the young, handsome ski instructors, while Sam and Jeff discussed where they wanted to go for dinner.

Suddenly Jeff yelled to Sam, "Watch out!" Sam turned around just in time to see a big, burly skier barreling toward him. It was too late to get out of the way, so Sam leaned back on his skis and braced for a collision. Luckily, the out-of-

70

control skier brushed past him, although he was so close that he zipped right over Sam's skis. "Hey, you idiot! Look out!" Sam yelled.

Hearing her brothers, Jackie turned around. To her horror, she realized she was directly in the skier's path. He was going so fast that Jackie didn't even have time to scream. The six-foot, 200-pound skier smashed into the slightly built, five-foot-two, 110-pound teenager with a sickening thud. The impact knocked off Jackie's hat, goggles, and gloves and sent her sprawling five feet into a snowbank.

Her brothers uncoupled their skis and raced over to their sister, who lay unconscious in the snow, her left leg at an odd angle. In a fit of anger, Jeff ran to the other skier, who was dusting himself off. "You lamebrain! Look what you did to my sister!"

"I'm sorry," the skier whined. "I couldn't turn. My knee locked up and I couldn't stop."

A crowd had gathered around Jackie. "Is she dead?" asked one skier. "I've never seen anybody hit that hard before," said another.

Although Jackie was seriously injured, it was not life-threatening, according to the doctors who treated her at the hospital emergency room. About two hours after the accident, Jackie woke up and found herself in a hospital bed, still groggy, her eyes struggling to focus on the faces in the room.

"Where am I?" she mumbled.

"You're in the hospital, honey," said her mother, leaning on the bed and tenderly brushing Jackie's long, blonde hair. "A speeding skier plowed into you."

"How do you feel?" asked her father.

"I hurt all over—my head, my ribs, my leg. What's wrong with me?"

"You have a broken leg and a possible concussion," her mother replied. "You'll have to spend a couple of days here."

"Oh, no," Jackie whimpered. "This vacation has been so great—and now it's turned into a nightmare."

"I know. It's a bad break."

But soon Jackie would discover that it was the luckiest break of her life.

A nurse walked up to Jackie's bed. "Hi. I'm Margie. So, you've decided to wake up, huh? Good. I'm going to give you some medication, but I don't want you getting out of bed. You had a nasty collision, and we want to make sure that you don't have anything more serious than a broken leg."

Later that evening, after the family left to get dinner, Margie returned to Jackie's room. "Jackie, you've been a bad girl," she said in a mocking tone.

"What did I do?"

"I saw you in your wheelchair rolling down the hall. I would've stopped you, but I had an emergency. Now, please, it's important that you stay put."

"Honest, Margie. I didn't go anywhere. I've been in this bed the whole time."

Margie nodded and winked as though she didn't believe Jackie. "Okay, okay. Just make sure you stay there."

A few minutes later, a lady with the dinner cart entered the room. As she put Jackie's plate on a tray, she gave the teenager a funny glance. "Didn't I just see you in a different room about twenty minutes ago?"

"No, not me. I've been here the whole time."

"You're the one who's allergic to milk, right?"

"Yeah, that's right," Jackie replied. "How did you know?"

"You told me."

"If I did, I don't remember. I have a slight concussion."

The next day, the doctor asked for another set of X rays, so Jackie was wheeled down to the radiology department. On her way, she stopped the meal lady and whispered, "Could you sneak me an extra piece of chocolate cake?"

"Of course, honey," the woman replied.

At the radiology department, the technician greeted Jackie. "Back again, huh?"

"Yeah. I guess they want an encore."

"So how is that boyfriend of yours?"

"Excuse me?"

"Your boyfriend. The one who brought you flowers."

"I doubt if my boyfriend even knows I'm in the hospital," said Jackie. "He's visiting friends in Ottawa."

"But I thought you told me your boyfriend brought flowers to decorate your wheelchair."

"You must have me confused with someone else."

"Well, I have been working double shifts," said the technician. "I'm obviously mistaken."

As she was wheeled back to her room, Jackie saw the meal lady passing out food trays. "Were you able to get me an extra piece of cake?" asked Jackie.

"I just gave it to you a few minutes ago."

"No, you didn't. I've been in radiology all morning. I'm just heading back to my room now."

The woman looked Jackie in the eyes and said, "Girl, do you have a twin in this hospital?"

Jackie laughed. "Nope. Just me, the one-and-only Jackie Langdon."

"If it's not your twin, then you've got a doppelganger—an exact double."

"Where did you last see her?"

"Over in the east wing, same floor."

Later that day, Jackie wheeled herself over to the east wing. Her leg was now in a cast, which her family and several nurses had already signed.

As she turned the corner, Dr. Bob Dotson, a young intern, came up to her and said, "Hi. I was just coming into your room to sign your cast." He patted his shirt pocket. "All I've got is a ballpoint pen. Let me get a marker."

I've never seen this doctor before in my life, Jackie thought. *Should I say something? Maybe I lost part of my memory from that concussion. I'm too embarrassed to tell him I don't know who he is.*

"Okay, I'm back," said the physician. He bent over to start writing, then hesitated. "Who's Jackie?"

"Me. Why?"

"All the autographs on this cast are to Jackie. What about Sheila?"

"Who's Sheila?"

"You are," the doctor claimed. "That's what it says on your chart. That's what we've been calling you. Sheila Walters."

"One of us is confused—and I hope it's you, or I'll be staying in this hospital to have my head examined. My name is Jackie Langdon."

"Do you have a twin sister here?"

"No, but I'm beginning to think there's a patient here who looks a lot like me."

"This is uncanny," marveled the doctor. "Stay right here. I'm going to check the medical records."

Moments after the intern walked off, Jackie spotted a blonde-haired girl wheeling herself down an intersecting corridor. Although Jackie was unable to see her features very clearly, she noticed the girl looked a lot like her. Jackie hurriedly rolled her wheelchair, trying to catch up. But when she turned the corner, the other girl was nowhere to be found.

After searching the area for a few minutes, Jackie started back to her room. Then she saw a glass-enclosed garden sunroom for patients and visitors and decided to go inside to admire the petunias, begonias, and lilies. Flowers always cheered her up.

"The begonias are looking pretty good, don't you think?"

Jackie turned to reply to the person behind her and gasped. She was staring into the face of a wheelchair-bound girl in a leg cast who looked exactly like Jackie. They shared the same features—long, silky blonde hair; blue-gray eyes; a small, slightly upturned nose; and dimpled cheeks.

"Are you Sheila Walters?" asked Jackie.

"Yes, I am. Who are you?"

"Jackie Langdon. My gosh, you look just like me."

"No, you look just like me," countered Sheila, with a wink and a grin. "We look like twins."

At the same moment, they asked each other, "When were you born?" They remained silent for a few seconds, awed by having spoken the same words at the same time.

Jackie, almost fearfully, said, "December 19, 1953."

Sheila screamed. "Oh, my gosh! That's my birthday, too!"

"I was born in Toronto."

"Me, too!"

"I was adopted," said Jackie.

Sheila grew silent. "I wasn't. I mean, my parents never said I was. I just assumed I was theirs."

"My parents—my adoptive parents, that is—never mentioned that my biological mother had any other kids," said Jackie.

"Could it be just a series of amazing coincidences?" Pointing to the three necklaces around Jackie's neck, Sheila said, "You wear three necklaces just like I do." Holding up her thumbs, she added, "And you have rings on your thumbs, just like me."

"What's your favorite color?" asked Jackie.

"Blue."

"Me, too! What's your favorite food?"

"Chocolate cake," replied Sheila.

"I love it more than anything!" Pointing to the cast on Sheila's left leg, Jackie asked, "So what happened to you?"

"A stupid skiing accident. I was riding the lift, and the skier in front of me fell while he was getting off. He was lying on the ramp, but the lift attendant didn't stop the lift. Instead, he tried to drag the fallen skier off to the side. Before they could get clear, my chair reached the unloading ramp. I tried to avoid them, but I fell and broke my leg. Pretty dumb, huh? What about you?"

"I was in a skiing accident, too. Some hotdog idiot rammed into me at the bottom of Bearwallow Run. I got a concussion and a broken leg."

"This is way too weird. Where do you live, Jackie?"

"In Brampton. What about you?"

"In Newmarket, not too far from you."

Just then, Dr. Dotson walked into the garden room, holding two folders. "There you are—my gosh, you're both here! It's amazing! You look like twins!"

"Yes," said Sheila, "but we can't be because—"

Dr. Dotson interrupted her. "I'm going over your medical records. Same date of birth, same blood type, same height and weight. I mean, everything is identical. Even your past medical history. You both have been treated for migraine headaches and for a childhood kidney problem that went away. Sheila, it says on your chart that you're allergic to milk. Jackie, are you?"

Jackie nodded. "And I can do this." She grabbed her thumb and pulled it back until it touched the back of her wrist.

"So can I," said Sheila, duplicating the feat.

"Do you have any special talents?" asked the doctor. "For example, do you play a musical instrument?"

"I used to play piano," said Jackie, "but I stopped when I was ten."

"Me, too!"

Just as remarkable, the girls discovered that they each owned a cat named Tiger, wore the same kind of perfume, loved flowers, enjoyed Chinese food, and liked the same music. They each had a boyfriend who was a goalie on the school soccer team.

"You must be twins," insisted the intern.

Jackie turned to Sheila and said, "Do you think we were separated at birth?"

"I don't know what to think. My parents never said I was adopted. But after seeing you . . ."

The girls went back to their rooms, after vowing to meet later that day with their parents in Sheila's room.

When Sheila returned to her room, her parents were there. "Mom, Dad, the most incredible thing has happened!" She excitedly launched into an account of her encounter with Jackie, barely stopping for a breath.

When she finally finished, she said, "Jackie wondered if we were separated at birth. She was adopted, but I wasn't, was I? You would've told me, right?"

At first, she was bewildered by the expression on her parents' faces. Her father looked anguished, and her mother was crying. Sheila trembled and burst into tears. "Oh, my gosh! I *was* adopted!"

"We were going to tell you, but it was so hard for us," said her mother. "We put it off and put it off, thinking you weren't old enough. Then one day you were old enough, but by then it seemed we had waited too long. We made a terrible, terrible mistake in not telling you sooner. Please forgive us."

"Then who is my biological mother?"

"We don't know. You came from an adoption agency. All we know is that the mother was a teenager who gave you up at birth. We weren't aware that you had a twin sister."

Just then, Jackie and her parents entered the room. Jackie's parents were astounded at seeing Sheila. "Oh, my goodness! It's true!" cried Jackie's mom. "You do have a twin sister!"

The two sets of parents compared notes and found that the girls came from the same adoption agency. Later, further investigation revealed that the agency had split up the infant twins without telling the adoptive parents.

"If we hadn't both broken our legs, we might have gone through our entire lives and never known about each other," said Sheila, squeezing her sister's hand.

"We can really say, 'We met by accident,'" cracked Jackie.

After the discovery, the girls stayed in close contact with each other. Along with their families, they met for dinner at least once a month.

At their first dinner together, the girls went to a Chinese restaurant and both ordered the same meal—cashew chicken. They also discovered they had received identical grades in the same school subjects for the latest grading period. At the end of the meal, everyone was given a fortune cookie.

Sheila opened hers first and laughed as she read it. "'You will find a long-lost relative who will bring you great joy.' Okay, Jackie. Top that one."

Jackie split her cookie and pulled out the fortune.

After silently reading it, she announced, "I think I can. My fortune says, 'Sometimes bad breaks bring good results.'"

Artful Destiny

"We've been invited back to Spring Fest," announced Myra Jensen. "Do we dare go?"

"Not without a police escort," her husband, Willy, replied. "After the bizarre things that happened to us the first two years at that art fair, I'm leery about going."

"But maybe that's why we should go—just to see what strange thing will happen to us this time. The coincidences have been amazing."

The Jensens' life revolved around art. She made sculptures; he made jewelry. They didn't earn a whole lot of money—just enough to live modestly in their quaint apartment. The place had a kitchen-dining-living area, a bedroom, a bathroom, and a glass-enclosed studio, where the Jensens created their works of art.

Both of the Jensens were in their twenties, and their looks sometimes confused strangers. Willy had long, dark hair that he kept in a ponytail. He was slightly built and wore baggy, loose-fitting clothes and a hoop earring. Myra, however, had buzzed her blonde hair. Although shorter, she was more muscular than her husband and dressed almost exclusively in overalls. More than once, people had mistaken Myra for the husband and Willy for the wife.

Willy worked mostly with silver, creating designs with such stones as amethyst, emerald, and turquoise. His jewelry had a unique, futuristic style that made it look like it should be worn by someone from the twenty-second century.

Depending on her mood, Myra sculpted in either clay or marble. If she was in an especially positive mood, she created exotic figures out of clay. "I like having the freedom to take a blob of clay and mold it into a character that exists deep within my soul," she once said. "I like the feel and texture of clay, to press my fingers into the mix and to pinch and pull and let them bring the figure to life." Whenever she felt an intense emotion, either good or bad, she liked sculpting in marble with her hammer and chisel. "The sculpture is already in the marble," she liked to say. "It's up to me to chip away until it emerges."

During the winter months, the Jensens worked side by side on their separate crafts, creating a large inventory that they sold to local stores. But every spring they traveled the art fair circuit. They piled their creations into the back of a cranky twenty-four-foot motor home and went from fair to fair, selling their art. Depending on the weather and the location, they could make decent money.

The Jensens would never forget the first time they signed on for Spring Fest. They loaded their RV, which they had named Venus—after the Roman goddess of love and beauty— and drove two hundred miles to the three-day event.

On the second day of the fair, an older gentleman with a flowing barbershop-style mustache that seemed as wide as his round face stopped by their booth. He eyed one particular sculpture of Myra's. Chiseled from a piece of black-and-pink marble, it had a haunting, angular face that seemed anguished. Seeing his interest, she walked over to him. "I'm quite fond of that piece," he said.

"Me, too," Myra replied. "I call it 'Woe.' I sculpted it after I had to put my cat to sleep."

The man looked at her with a raised eyebrow. "Most people who are trying to sell something probably wouldn't be talking about dead cats."

"I want my art to express the truth. I don't know any other way."

"The truth is that this is an excellent piece," he said. "Believe it or not, the word 'woe' entered my mind the moment I saw it."

"Are you going to buy it? The price is five hundred dollars."

The man handed her a business card. "My name is Bernard Hyde, owner of the Morning Sun Gallery. My wife is one of the organizers of this art fair. A customer of mine is quite an art lover. Unfortunately, he's bedridden at the moment. I think if I show him this piece, he'll buy it. Do you mind if I take it to him? If he doesn't buy it, I'll return it tomorrow."

"What will you get out of this, a commission?"

Mr. Hyde shook his head. "No, it would be my pleasure to find a beautiful piece of art for a good client and to help a young, talented artist like you."

Myra studied him for a moment and said, "You look trustworthy. Okay."

She carefully wrapped the sculpture in paper and put it in a wooden box as they exchanged idle chatter.

"Is that your motor home?" he asked.

"Yeah, that's Venus. We're staying over at the campground at the state park." She handed him the sculpture. "I hope your client likes this piece. Please be careful with it. If there's any damage, it's yours for life. Have a nice day, Mr. Hyde."

After he left, Myra told Willy, "I have a feeling this is going to be a great fair for us."

The Jensens sold several more pieces that day. By the time night fell, they had loaded the remaining artwork into Venus and driven to the campground.

About two in the morning, a spring shower pelted their motor home, waking Myra. She was just drifting back to sleep when she heard a car roar down the campground road. She didn't think much of it—until she heard a loud thump, as though something had been tossed out of the car. She sat up and looked out the window but couldn't see anything in the darkness.

At daybreak, Myra got up and stepped outside for a walk in the morning mist. About ten feet from the motor home, she saw a shattered wooden box and a pink-and-black object lying in the mud. She plucked it from the muck, brushed it off, and shouted, "Willy! Willy! Get out here!"

Willy could tell from Myra's voice that she was extremely upset. He tumbled out of bed and burst out of the RV. "What's wrong?"

"Look!" she said, holding up the object.

Through his sleepy eyes and the mist, he said, "That looks like the sculpture you gave the gallery owner yesterday."

"That's because it *is* the sculpture! Do you believe the nerve of that guy? A car roared through here last night, and then I heard something hit the ground. That jerk Mr. Hyde just tossed the sculpture out of his car. Thank goodness it's not damaged."

"How did he know where to throw it?"

"He saw the motor home behind our booth, and I told him where we were camping. When he took the sculpture, he said he'd bring it back if his client didn't want it. But I never imagined he would think so little of this piece that he'd throw it in the dirt! Oh, I'm so mad, I'd like to give him a piece of my mind. It's absolutely outrageous!"

Willy took the sculpture from Myra's shaking hands. "I'll clean it up," he said. "He's a Class-A moron. You have a right to be ticked off. Why don't you go for a walk and cool down? I'll make us some coffee."

Myra went stomping off into the mist. An hour later, she was still peeved over the incident.

When they returned to the fair, Myra kept her eyes peeled, hoping that she would spot Mr. Hyde so she could chew him out. Late that afternoon, she was wrapping up another sale when the art dealer stepped into the booth.

Fearing that Myra would start yelling at Mr. Hyde and chase all the customers away, Willy dashed out from behind his display case and gently grabbed his wife. "Why don't you go out behind the tent and talk—not too loudly—to this creep."

Shooting darts with her eyes at Mr. Hyde, Myra motioned for him to follow her to the back. Behind the tent, Mr. Hyde hemmed and hawed. "I don't know how to say this—"

"Well, then I will," snapped Myra. "You are a real jerk!

What was going through your head?"

"I know. I was wrong. It was so dumb of me."

"Dumb? It was more than dumb! It was rude and crude and just plain disgusting."

"Well, I don't know if I'd go that far, but . . . wait a second. How did you know about the sculpture?"

"How did I know? You threw it in the mud next to my motor home last night. Hey, if your client didn't like it, fine. But did you have to hurl it out of your car?"

"What?" Mr. Hyde cried out. "I don't know what you're talking about. I came to apologize for doing a dumb thing. After I left here yesterday with the sculpture, I bought a few other pieces and put them in the backseat of my car. On the way home, I stopped at a restaurant and foolishly forgot to lock the doors. As I was walking back, I saw the doors to my car were open. Two men were getting into a bright red Jeep Cherokee that was parked next to my car. They took off, but I got their license plate number. When I looked in my car, everything was gone—my camera and all the artwork, including your sculpture. I called the police. Sometime during the night, they spotted the Jeep and gave chase. They caught the guys in the park, but when the officers searched the car, they didn't find anything. The sculpture is gone."

Myra broke out in a broad grin and placed her hand on his shoulder. "Mr. Hyde, you're not going to believe this. Follow me." She led him back into the tent and pointed to a pedestal.

"The sculpture!" he exclaimed. "But how . . . why . . . ?"

"It's an incredible coincidence. While the robbers were being chased through the park, they threw the sculpture out of their car—right in front of my motor home!"

"Unbelievable!"

"Do you still want the sculpture?"

"Yes! Of course."

"I'll give it to you on one condition," she said. "Keep it locked in the trunk and drive straight to your client's house!"

Mr. Hyde did just that and returned later with five hundred dollars.

What happened to the Jensens the following year at Spring Fest was just as startling—if not more so.

They had done a brisk business the first two days, but for some reason Sunday was slower. Early in the afternoon, Myra decided to get lunch for the two of them, leaving Willy alone in the booth.

About two minutes later, two men in their early twenties wearing black baseball caps, sunglasses, sport shirts, and khakis walked into the tent with a tall, thin, teenage girl with straight brown hair. The girl, who had rings pierced through her cheeks and nose, was wearing an ankle-length, blue-and-white tie-dyed dress.

The girl and one of the men were admiring one of Myra's smaller clay sculptures that carried a price tag marked $150. "Excuse me, sir," said the man. "How firm is the price?"

"Well, we'll be closing up soon," said Willy. "I can knock twenty-five dollars off. But that's it."

"Would you take one hundred dollars for it?" Just then the girl's hand accidentally hit the sculpture, knocking it off its stand. With catlike quickness, her companion dove to the ground and managed to catch the falling sculpture in his hands.

"Great save!" yelled a relieved Willy, as he raced from

behind his display counter. The man handed him the sculpture and then winced in pain. "I think I jammed my knee," he moaned, still sitting on the ground.

Willy bent down. "Is there anything I can do?"

"No, but thanks anyway. I'll be all right." He winced again. Then, with the girl's help, he stood up and said, "I hope your sculpture is okay."

Willy checked and was relieved when he couldn't find any nicks or cracks on the sculpture. "It looks fine. Thanks so much for saving it. Man, you have great reflexes. If I didn't know better, I'd say you were waiting for it to fall. Tell you what. For your good deed, I'll sell it to you for one hundred dollars."

The man turned to the girl and asked, "What do you think?"

She shook her head and said, "I don't think so. Let's keep looking."

The man shrugged and then walked out of the tent with her.

"Hey," said Willy, "thanks for saving the sculpture."

Moments later, Myra returned with lunch. As they walked toward their chairs behind the jewelry counter, she stopped and stared at the glass case. "My gosh, Willy. Either you just made a great sale or—"

"Oh, no!" Willy cried. "We've been robbed!" The case had been completely cleaned out of all the remaining jewelry—at least twenty pieces worth more than five hundred dollars.

"I was duped big time," he muttered. "I fell for one of the oldest scams in the book. Two young guys and a body-pierced girl came in. One of the men and the girl distracted me, and I totally forgot about the other guy. He must have slipped behind me, emptied out the display case, and then disappeared out the back of the tent." Willy smacked his clenched left fist into the palm of his right hand. "There went all our profit for the weekend."

The Jensens quickly reported the theft to the police, but they knew there was little chance the thieves would be caught. Glumly, they closed their tent early, packed the motor home, and, with Myra at the wheel, headed toward home in silence.

After half an hour on the road, Willy said, "I'm going in the back to take a nap and try to sleep away all these bad feelings I have."

About ten minutes later, Myra saw a pickup truck on the shoulder of the road. A teenage girl in a blue-and-white tie-dyed dress was bent over the rear tire, which was flat. Myra stopped beside the truck and got out of the motor home. "Need help?" she asked the girl.

"Yeah. I don't have a spare," said the girl.

"How about if I give you a lift to the next town?"

"Oh, that would be great. Thanks. Um, do you mind if my friends come, too?"

Out from the bushes walked two young men in black baseball caps, sport shirts, and khakis. They politely tipped their caps. The taller man said, "If you feel uncomfortable about taking three strangers, we understand. But it's Sunday, and we might not get any help until tomorrow."

"No problem," said Myra. "Come on in."

"That's very kind."

As the three climbed in, Myra's eyes suddenly focused on the silver bracelets they were wearing. Then she gazed at their earrings, and their rings and necklaces. She had seen all the jewelry before—they were the very items that had been stolen hours earlier!

Her heart racing, Myra tried hard not to change expression or let on in any way that she knew they were the culprits. "I'll be right back," Myra told them. "I want to wake up my husband, so he doesn't get alarmed when he sees three strangers in our motor home."

While the thieves made themselves comfortable, Myra entered the bedroom and sat on the edge of the bed where Willy was napping. "Willy," she whispered, shaking him awake. "Guess who's in our motor home? The three thieves!"

"What?" he yelped, bolting up, only to have Myra throw her hand over his mouth.

"Hush," she said. "I don't want them to hear you. Their truck has a flat tire, and I offered them a lift. I didn't realize they were the crooks until they got in and I saw they were wearing your jewelry."

Quickly the Jensens created a plan. Myra returned to the front of the motor home and told them, "My husband is sick, so forgive him for not coming out. But you wouldn't want to catch what he's got."

She moved into the driver's seat and started the engine. "There's soda in the refrigerator if you'd like."

"Man, this is great," said one of the men. "It's like fate sent you to us."

Myra laughed heartily. "Boy, you don't know how right you are."

As the motor home entered the next town, Willy stepped out from the bedroom and said, "Well, hello there. I remember you. You're the three who came into my tent to admire my wife's sculpture—and steal my jewelry."

"Oh, no," whined the girl. "Are you kidding me? What are the odds of this happening? Oh, man."

"I think it would be wise to hand over my jewelry right now. All of it."

"Hey, there are three of us and only two of you," said one of the men. "What do you think you can do to us?"

"I wouldn't try anything if I were you," Myra warned. "Look where we are." She had just turned the motor home into the parking lot of the police department, where the three were promptly arrested.

"Do you really want to go to Spring Fest for a third time?" Willy asked Myra. "The first year, thieves toss your sculpture right in our campsite. Last year, thieves literally walk into our motor home with our stolen goods. Should we chance it?"

"Let's do it!" Myra suggested. "I can't wait to see what will happen next."

Fortunately, no crimes were committed at Spring Fest that year. Nothing extraordinary happened that required fate to step in—unless, of course, you count what Willy found on the ground a few feet away from their tent at the fair. It was a lost credit card belonging to none other than Mr. Bernard Hyde.

Helping Hands

Zack Austin aimlessly strolled through the mall, staying several steps ahead of his mother, Kim. It wasn't cool for a twelve-year-old to be seen in public with his mother.

Suddenly, panic hijacked Zack's body. His heart pounded like a frenzied rock-band drummer. An invisible vise squeezed his chest, causing him to gasp for breath. At the same time, the mall's center court started spinning in sync with his tumbling stomach. Frantically, the terror-stricken boy staggered to the nearest bench and collapsed. Grabbing the wooden bench with his clammy hands, his body flushed and sweaty, Zack closed his eyes and pressed his face hard against the slats.

Kim raced over to her son, put her arms around him, and said softly, "I'm here, honey. I'm here."

The two of them had lived this frightening episode many times before in other locations—the nature center, the post office, the amusement park. Zack suffered from strange panic attacks, during which an inexplicable fear would seize him. He never knew what it was or where it came from. The panic would just happen. And it would be intense.

Whenever Zack suffered a panic attack, his whole body reacted as if he were trapped in a cage with the world's most horrible, bloodthirsty monster. There was nothing he could do except ride the treacherous wave of fear. Within a few minutes, his body would relax and the nervousness would ease. Then, as he regained his senses and his breathing returned to normal, Zack would notice a crowd of strangers staring at him, and he'd feel an uncomfortable rush of embarrassment.

Following the incident at the mall, Zack's panic attacks increased in intensity until the fear of having one left him homebound. He eventually refused to go to school, because he couldn't leave his house without being stricken by crippling anxiety. Zack's parents sought the help of several doctors, who diagnosed his problem as panic with agoraphobia—the fear of being in a public place. They prescribed various medications, but nothing seemed to help.

Then fate stepped in—twice—to help turn Zack's life around.

One snowy day, about a year after Zack's panic attack at the mall, his father, Hank, was on the job, dropping off and picking up packages for a delivery service. The streets were quite dangerous, because a few inches of snow had fallen on top of a thick layer of ice. Although the snowplows were running twenty-four hours a day, they had yet to clear many of the slick side roads.

Hank tried driving up a hill to reach one rural address, but his tires started spinning about halfway up, and he had to back down the road. Company policy said that if weather conditions were bad, the driver didn't have to make the delivery. Hank eyed the return address and saw the package was from a catalog house. It wasn't anything crucial—like a legal document, a check, or medicine. It wasn't anything that couldn't wait another day. And yet, Hank was determined to deliver the package.

Guessing that the address was about an eighth of a mile away, Hank hopped out of his truck and began the trek to the house. As he trudged to the top of the hill, he heard several ducks quacking on a nearby frozen pond. Across the street, a golden retriever puppy played in the snow with a preschooler bundled in a snowsuit.

Hank smiled. *Wouldn't it be great if Zack could one day be as carefree and happy as that child is?* he thought wistfully. The delivery man passed a few more houses and then reached the address. When he handed over the package to an elderly woman, she was thrilled because it was a birthday gift for her neighbor. She insisted Hank take several fresh-baked cookies as thanks for hiking up the hill to deliver it.

As Hank walked back, munching on the warm cookies, he heard a frantic voice shouting, "Charlotte! Charlotte! Where are you?" A woman was running around the front of the house where Hank had seen the child and the dog playing. He dashed over to the woman, whose face was streaked with fear. "I can't find my daughter! She was here just a second ago playing with her puppy!"

"I'll check across the street." Then Hank noticed that the puppy, wet and barking, was standing at the edge of the pond. He raced over and found a child's footprints leading onto the frozen pond. About ten yards out, he saw a hole in the ice. A head bobbed to the surface and then went under.

"She fell in the pond!" Hank yelled. "Call 911!" He quickly got on his belly and began crawling out on the ice, but it cracked under his weight and gave way. Although the water was only a few feet deep, its bitter cold left him in near shock. He thrashed through the ice and freezing water, hoping against hope that the little girl would surface again. But Charlotte didn't. *I've only got a few seconds to find her!* Hank thought. Frantically he groped around, trying to feel for the body. *Where is she?* Then his knee hit a soft object. He reached down and pulled up the unconscious child. "I've got her! I've got her!"

Holding Charlotte to his chest, Hank waded back through the broken ice to where several neighbors had gathered. As he laid the little girl on the ground, Charlotte began coughing and crying.

"Thank goodness!" he cheered. "She's breathing!"

Her mother rushed over, held her tight, and wept with joy and relief. "Oh, Charlotte, Charlotte!"

"I'm sorry, Mommy," the little girl whimpered. "I was playing with Trixie, and she ran after a duck, and I chased her on the ice, and then I fell in."

The woman turned to the now-shivering Hank and hugged him. "How can I ever repay you?"

"Seeing her alive is payment enough," he told her.

A few days after the rescue, Charlotte's parents, Dr. Jon Demeter and his wife, Sarah, invited Hank and his family over for dinner. Hank and Kim came without Zack, who refused to leave the house.

During their meal, Hank asked Dr. Demeter what kind of medicine he practiced. "I'm a psychiatrist specializing in anxiety disorders," he replied. "Are you familiar with them?"

Kim and Hank dropped their forks and stared in open-mouthed amazement at each other. "Familiar with them?" Hank said. "We live with them. Our son, Zack, suffers from panic attacks and agoraphobia. For nearly a year, Zack hasn't been able to walk out his front door for fear of being away from his safety net, and for fear of being embarrassed. He can't stand in the lunch line at school without feeling faint. He'll get a sudden urge to go to the bathroom and be terrified that he can't make it in time. He's consumed with what-ifs: 'What if I panic and go crazy? What if I panic and someone sees me? What if I panic and pass out?' The what-ifs play over and over in his mind until the anxiety keeps him homebound."

Kim looked directly into Dr. Demeter's eyes and added, "We've tried everything and been everywhere hoping to get help. We're at our wits' end."

Dr. Demeter leaned over the table and gently squeezed Kim's hand. "Your husband saved our daughter. Let me return the favor by trying to save your son."

Through a combination of medication, therapy, and diet, Zack was successfully treated for his frightening disorder. Under Dr. Demeter's care, the boy began venturing out into the real world and took the first steps to returning to a normal life. But he still had a major hurdle to clear.

During treatment, Dr. Demeter discovered that Zack suffered from a learning disability that teachers and school officials had failed to detect. The disability was the likely trigger for Zack's panic disorder and needed to be treated by specialists.

The Austins searched for a private school that would accept Zack. But because of his learning disability and his medical record, every school he applied to rejected him. "Classes start in two weeks, and we don't have a school for him," Kim complained to Hank. "What can we do?"

"Where's the best school for Zack?" he asked her.

"Dunwoody. It's not far from here, and it has an excellent reputation. But they won't take him, because they're afraid Zack will have a relapse. They don't want to be responsible if anything happens to him."

"Ask them again."

"I already asked twice, and they said no."

"We'll think of something. Never give up." Hank looked at the kitchen clock. "Say, aren't you supposed to be getting ready for that charity fashion show?"

"Yes, but I don't feel like going. I'm so upset."

"Go. It will do you good."

Reluctantly, Kim went. As it turned out, the entire Austin family was very glad she did.

Kim arrived late for the event, which was held at a swank country club. When she entered the dining room, she surveyed the two dozen large tables, trying to decide where to sit. Most of the tables had at least one empty seat. *Just pick a table*, Kim told herself. Almost blindly, she walked over to a table of older, extremely well-dressed women and took the lone empty seat. As soon as she sat down, Kim asked herself, *Why didn't I choose a table with women closer to my own age? I can't get up now; I'll look foolish. I'm stuck with them. I hope I can find something to talk about with these women.*

She politely introduced herself to everyone and was

relieved to find them quite friendly. During the fashion show, she hit it off with the person next to her, Margaret Johnson. Margaret, a matronly and obviously wealthy woman, wore her pearls and other jewelry with elegance, but she didn't act snooty. After the fashion show ended, almost everyone left, but the two continued to chat.

When the conversation turned to education, Kim couldn't resist telling Margaret about Zack and the difficulty of trying to get him into a private school that specialized in learning-disabled students. As she continued to reveal her situation to Margaret, Kim thought, *This woman doesn't want to hear your troubles. You don't even know her. She's probably itching to get out of here. Stop now!* But Kim couldn't. She was on a roll, and she had nowhere else to turn. Finally, when she had finished her heartfelt monologue about Zack, Kim put her hands to her face and began to blush.

"Oh, Margaret, I'm so ashamed of myself. I've just poured out my problems to you, and that's probably the last thing you wanted to hear today. Please forgive me, but you've been such a gracious listener, and I—"

Margaret cut her off. "Kim, you're in luck," she said warmly, "because you told your story to the right person. It just so happens that I am a close friend of the director of Dunwoody. Not only that, but I am a major contributor to the school and have raised a great deal of money for the place. You can consider Zack a new Dunwoody student. I'll get him in. I give you my word."

Tears trickled down Kim's face. She reached over and clasped the woman's hands. "Oh, Margaret, thank you, thank you," she cried.

As promised, Margaret convinced the director of Dunwoody to accept Zack into the school. After a rough few weeks of adjusting, Zack began to thrive. In fact, he did so well that he made the honor roll by the end of the second grading period.

Forever grateful, Kim stayed in touch with Margaret, sending her cards and notes. Every so often, Margaret would call, inquiring about Zack's progress.

About two years later, Margaret was honored for all the charities she helped fund. When Kim went to the reception, she was in for a shocking surprise.

As the ceremony began, Kim noticed a woman about her own age standing next to Margaret, holding her hand. Kim was sure she had met the younger woman before but couldn't quite place where.

During a lull in the proceedings, Kim turned to the person next to her and whispered, "Pardon me, but do you know who the woman is standing at Margaret's left?"

"That's her daughter, Paula. She has a mental disability, but she's very sweet, very loving."

Kim reeled from the answer. A chill wound its way up her spine. Now she remembered where she had met Paula—eighteen years ago at Brevard High, a private school.

Kim's mind raced back to her senior year, when Paula, who had Down's Syndrome, joined her class. Paula's arrival stirred controversy among the administration and even among some students and their parents. The school didn't have any teachers trained to handle special-needs students. But after her wealthy parents pulled a few strings and made a generous donation, officials somewhat reluctantly allowed Paula to enroll.

Paula was placed in Kim's class, where most of the students, through ignorance, did not treat her with the dignity and respect she deserved. They shunned her and made jokes about her behind her back.

Seeing how cruel the other students were to Paula, Kim took it upon herself to be the new girl's friend. They ate lunch together, and Kim helped her with her homework during study hall. Over the next few months, with Kim's daily prodding, the other students began to see that Paula was an eager student and a likable person.

But when it came time for the senior class trip to Washington, D.C., no one wanted to room with Paula at the hotel. So Kim volunteered. It wasn't easy, because it was one of the few times that Paula had ever been away from home, and she cried from homesickness. Kim stayed with her, which meant that she couldn't join in the after-curfew fun that the other kids enjoyed in their rooms. But when the class returned home, Kim felt glad that she had been Paula's buddy on the trip.

During the school year, Kim never had the chance to meet Paula's mother. After graduation, Kim lost touch with Paula, even though they both had remained in town.

Not until the ceremony honoring Margaret Johnson did Kim realize the extent to which destiny had played a hand in bringing their lives together. Kim had helped Margaret's daughter years ago, and now Margaret had helped Kim's son.

When she got to the front of the reception line, Kim congratulated Margaret on her charity work. "I'm delighted you came, Kim," Margaret said. "How's Zack doing?"

"Great, Margaret. Absolutely great, thanks to you."

"Isn't it a stroke of good fortune that you wound up sitting next to me at that fashion show?"

Before Kim could answer, Margaret put her arm around Paula and said, "Oh, Kim, I'd like you to meet my daughter, Paula."

Kim hugged Paula and asked her, "Do you remember me? We were classmates in high school."

Paula beamed and nodded. "You were my friend."

"Yes," said Kim. "And you were my friend."

"You know each other?" Margaret asked in astonishment.

"That's right, Margaret," Kim replied. "And now that I've learned who your daughter is, I'm convinced luck had nothing to do with my meeting you."

Katie's Lifesavers

Nineteen-year-old Katie Trantham looked at the platform 120 feet above her head. In a few minutes, she planned to hurl herself off that platform—the height of a twelve-story building. She would fall headfirst with nothing to save her from certain death but a thick elastic cord attached to her legs.

She had come to the county fair for no other reason than to try bungee jumping.

"Aren't you terrified?" asked her best friend, Rena Harrison.

"No, not really," replied Katie. "Whenever I've faced danger—whether planned or accidental—I've been saved by a twist of fate. Rena, you've been saved by that same fate at least once, remember?"

"It's time to cut the hay field," Claude Trantham announced to his four children and his wife at the breakfast table. "So everyone stay clear of the field."

Six-year-old Katie, as usual, wasn't paying much attention.

She was daydreaming about what it would be like to fly like the red-winged blackbird that was chirping on the fence outside the window.

"Matty," Claude said to his wife, "make sure Katie isn't playing in the field today."

"Don't worry. She's going over to Rena's house this morning, aren't you, Katie?"

"Huh?" the little girl murmured, still clinging to her daydream. "Why can't people fly?"

After breakfast, Matty walked Katie across the gravel road that separated the Tranthams' farm from the Harrisons' spread. Rena—who was also six years old—and Katie played together almost every day after they had completed their chores. In this part of Illinois, kids were never too young to help on the farm.

After amusing themselves with Rena's newest kittens, the two brown-haired pixies decided to walk across the road and play hide-and-seek in the Tranthams' hay field, where the stalks stood a foot taller than they were.

While they frolicked in the field, Claude was next to the barn, attaching an eight-foot-wide band of steel cutters to the front of his tractor. Then he started up the engine and headed toward the field. The girls were still playing among the hay stalks as Claude—unaware of them—motored up and down the field, cutting down wide swaths with each pass.

After a while, the girls quit playing hide-and-seek, but they still remained hidden in the hay. "Let's pretend we're bunnies and the tractor is a big, bad wolf," said Katie.

"Okay," said Rena. "And we can't go anywhere that's been cut. We have to stay in the tall stalks."

For the next thirty minutes, the girls darted to and fro

among the hay stalks, too small to be seen by Claude. The noise of the tractor grew louder as the remaining patch of hay shrank with each pass. Finally, Claude had only one small strip left to mow in the middle of the field—the strip that concealed two little girls. They sat giggling in the stalks, totally oblivious to the looming danger.

The sharp, deadly blades effortlessly chopped down the hay as the tractor closed in on the girls. Twenty yards away . . . fifteen yards . . . ten yards. Suddenly, the tractor engine coughed, sputtered, and died. Claude grunted and tried to start the engine, but it wouldn't turn over.

"That darn fuel line must be clogged again," he muttered out loud. "Shoot, I was almost finished." He slapped his hat against his knee in disgust. Then he heard girlish laughter in the stalks in front of him.

"Katie? Is that you?"

The giggling girls sprang to their feet and emerged from the tall hay only inches away from the cutter. "Surprise, Daddy!" yelled Katie.

Claude gasped, his face contorted in anger over the girls' recklessness and relief that they weren't harmed. He picked up both girls, hugged them, and began to cry.

"Did we scare you, Daddy?"

"Yes, you scared me so much that I feel like I died a thousand deaths," he wept. Claude knew that if it hadn't been for his engine conking out at that exact moment, his hay field would have turned into a tragic killing field.

"Rena, why don't you bungee jump, too?" Katie urged.

"No way, I'm chicken."

"It'll be fun. Come on, we always do crazy things together."

"Like the time we tried to parachute from a tree?"

"Yeah, well, um . . . no."

"You almost died, remember?"

"Yes, but fate was looking out for me."

On a sunny fall afternoon, Katie and Rena were running past the barn. Each girl was holding a folded bedsheet that trailed from the back of her neck like a cape.

"I'm Super Woman!" shouted Katie.

"And I'm Super Lady!" yelled Rena, scampering past Katie through the fallen leaves. The eight-year-olds' pretending had turned into a furious race that didn't stop until they reached a post along the Trantham farm's barbed-wire fence. "I win!" declared Rena. "Super Lady is queen!"

"You had a head start. That's not fair. If we could fly, I'd beat you every time." Katie leaned against a tall oak tree, trying to catch her breath. She casually gazed up at the tree, its thick branches spreading out so far they extended over the fence by the gravel road. Then an idea clicked in her head.

"Hey, Rena, let's climb the tree and then jump down. We'll use our sheets as parachutes!"

"Won't we get hurt?"

"Naw. We'll pile a bunch of leaves under the tree and fall on them."

After they had gathered the leaves, Katie wrapped the sheet around her waist and began climbing up the tree. Rena reluctantly followed.

When they were about ten feet up, Rena refused to go any farther. "This is plenty high for me." She carefully worked her way out on a branch, opened up the sheet, grabbed all four corners, and then jumped. Rena landed in the pile of leaves and rolled off onto the ground, splattering mud on her sweatshirt and jeans.

"How was it?" asked Katie.

"We need about a ton more leaves, because I hurt my ankle. It's too dangerous."

"I'll parachute down."

"You're too high, Katie. Please climb down. At least jump from my branch."

Just then a car honked and slowed to a stop. The driver lowered his window, stuck his head out, and said to Rena, "Excuse me, but I'm lost. I'm looking for the Taylor farm."

"The Taylors? They're about two miles from here. You go down this—"

A loud crack interrupted her. She looked up at the tree and screamed. The branch that Katie was on had snapped, sending her in a downward tumble. She struck another branch, which flipped her onto her back before she plunged straight onto the barbed-wire fence and then crashed to the ground.

Katie lay unconscious, blood flowing from a terrible gash on her right leg. The man leaped out of the car and raced over to her. Turning to Rena, he barked, "Run to the nearest house and call nine-one-one. I'll stay here with her."

While Rena took off, the man discovered that the barbed wire had ripped open Katie's right leg, severing a major artery. Knowing she had only a few minutes to live if he didn't stop the bleeding, he whipped off his tie and wrapped it tight above the cut.

Ten minutes later, Claude, Matty, and Rena arrived. "Oh,

my baby! My baby!" cried Matty, kneeling next to the still-unconscious girl.

"Please don't touch her," said the man. "She might have a spinal injury."

"Who are you?" Matty asked warily.

"I'm Dr. Len Granville. I was looking for the Taylor farm and I got lost. I stopped to talk to this girl here," he said, pointing to Rena, "when your daughter fell out of the tree and hit the barbed-wire fence. She cut open the main artery to her right leg. I had to put a tourniquet on it to stop the bleeding as quickly as possible."

Matty burst into sobs. "Thank goodness you were lost. My Katie might have died if you hadn't been here. We never would've been able to reach her in time, and hardly anyone travels on this road, so no one else could have helped."

Katie nudged Rena as they recalled the accident. "I was lucky," Katie said emphatically. "No broken bones or anything. The doctor happened to be at the right place at the right time."

"Oh, look," said Rena, pointing to the bungee platform. "Frankie is getting ready to jump. There he goes!"

"Aaahhh!" yelled their friend, as he leaped off the platform. He made a perfect swan dive, then plummeted toward an inflatable cushion. About twenty feet above the ground, the bungee cord stretched as far as it could before snapping Frankie back up. The crowd roared its approval.

"Oh, I can't wait to do it," Katie gushed.

"Isn't there any way I can talk you out of it?" Rena asked. "Haven't you received any warning signs, like—"

"Like the barn incident? No."

Fourteen-year-old Katie led her brown-and-black horse, Beau, into the barn after their afternoon ride was cut short by a torrential thunderstorm. She put him in the stall, but as she began brushing him, Beau neighed, whinnied, and stomped his feet.

"Easy, Beau," she said. "You're awfully skittish. It's just a little summer rain."

She scratched Beau's ear and rubbed his nose, hoping to calm him. But he still acted extremely jumpy. "I guess I'll stay with you until this storm passes. I'll go up in the loft and get some more hay for you."

Just then a gust of wind flung open the barn door, causing Beau to whinny as hay swirled throughout the barn. Katie covered her eyes, scurried to the front, and tried to close the door, but the wind had ripped off the latch. It took her a few minutes to repair the latch and secure the door. "There, that's fixed, Beau. Are you feeling better?"

Beau didn't act like he was. He kept pawing and neighing. "Now what was I going to do? Oh, yes, get you some fresh hay from the loft."

As she started for the ladder, a saddle fell off the peg on the wall. "Gee, this place is falling apart," Katie said. The saddle had been hooked on a peg that had inexplicably broken off. She tried to fix it but couldn't.

Since it was still raining hard outside, Katie killed time by cleaning and polishing the leather on her saddle. She sang lullabies to Beau, hoping to soothe him, but it wasn't doing much good. "I've never seen you act so weird," she told him. "You've been through lots of storms before. Oh, geez, you're probably fussing because you want hay. I'm sorry, I forgot about it. I'll get you some right now."

She gripped the wooden ladder fastened to the wall and began climbing. But when she reached the fourth rung, it split in two, and she slipped down. Unfortunately, when she tried to break her slide, she caught a nasty sliver that tore deep into the meaty part of her right hand.

"Oh, man, it feels like a dagger in there. Beau, I'm sorry, but I have to run to the house and get this taken care of. I'll be back later."

She bolted through the rain to the house, where her mother tended to her wound. "That's one of the worst slivers I've ever seen," Matty said with a whistle.

"As soon as the rain lets up, I'll go back to the barn and get some hay for Beau," Katie said. "He's been acting really strange. I guess the storm is making him nervous."

About twenty minutes later, Katie was getting ready to return to the barn when two sheriff's cars pulled up. Deputy Newt Powell got out and walked up to the house.

"Hello, Newt," said Matty. "How are you?"

"Not too well. I don't mean to alarm you, but we're looking for an escaped convict. Have you seen a dark-haired man in his twenties wearing a blue shirt and blue pants? He's about six feet tall and one hundred seventy-five pounds."

Matty shook her head and turned to Katie. "Have you, honey?"

"Nope. What'd he do?"

"He's in for murder," the deputy replied. "He's very dangerous. He got loose when the prison bus veered off the road into a ditch near here. Please keep all your doors locked and don't go anywhere alone. We'll catch this guy soon. Mind if we take a look in your barn?"

"He's not in there," Katie asserted. "I just came from the barn about twenty minutes ago."

"We'll take a look anyway."

A few minutes later, Katie peered out the window and screamed with alarm. "Mom! Look!"

Matty rushed to the window. Outside, two deputies were escorting a squirming, yelling, handcuffed man out of the barn. After the man was shoved into the back of the patrol car, Newt came back to the house to talk to Matty and Katie.

"We got our man," he announced. "He'd been hiding in your hayloft for the past couple of hours."

"Ooohhh!" shrieked Katie. "I was in the barn when he was there! So that's why Beau was fidgety. I thought it was the storm, but it was because the murderer was up in the loft. Ooohhh! What's really scary is that I tried to go up in the loft at least three times, but I always got sidetracked by something."

"That something," said Matty, "was fate."

"So who's next to take this test of bravery and have the thrill of a lifetime?" the bungee jumpmaster shouted to the crowd.

"I am!" declared Katie. "I'm ready to bungee jump!"

After paying her money and signing a legal document saying she knew of the risks, she climbed into the elevator that would take her to the platform twelve stories above.

"Be careful, Katie, please!" begged Rena.

"I'll be fine. And you'll be next!"

After moving up only three feet, the elevator sputtered

and stopped. Soon the workers ordered Katie to jump down. "It's going to take a while," the jumpmaster said. "Why don't you come back later? I'm sorry."

"I can't wait," said Katie. "We have a party to go to. Just give me back my money. I'll try tomorrow."

As the two girls returned to their car, Katie told Rena, "I'm really bummed out. I didn't want Frankie to be the only one of our crowd to bungee jump. He'll be boasting about it all night at the party."

"It's just as well," said Rena. "Maybe the broken elevator was a warning sign that you weren't supposed to bungee jump."

"Or maybe it was just a broken elevator and nothing more."

Later, on their way to the party, the girls turned the car radio to a rock station that was broadcasting from the fair. "I'm sad to report that there's been a terrible accident here at the fair," the DJ said somberly. "A man was seriously injured moments ago attempting to bungee jump, when the cord broke during his fall. Witnesses said the man, whose name has not been released, had reached the bottom of his drop when the cord broke. He plunged twenty feet to a cushion that helped break his fall. He was rushed to Good Samaritan Hospital. Apparently the attraction had been closed for nearly an hour because of a mechanical problem. The victim was the first to try the bungee jump after it reopened."

Upon hearing the news, Rena slammed on the brakes. She turned to her shocked friend and said, "That could have been you. If that elevator hadn't—"

"Yeah, I know," admitted Katie. "It looks like fate saved my life once again."

The Captain's Portrait

Early one spring morning, Ron Tobin was in-line skating on Kimberly Avenue, a quiet, shady street in Portland, Maine. Suddenly, a beagle charged out from behind a house. The dog howled and barked and took aim at the thirty-eight-year-old man.

Ron glanced over his shoulder, saw the dog bearing down on him, and sped up. Then, looking straight ahead, he gasped. A car was backing out of the driveway directly in front of him. With a thud, Ron slammed into the side, bounced off, and fell on his rear. The dazed skater crawled over to the curb and bent over, trying to catch his breath. Meanwhile, the beagle stopped chasing him but continued to bark and howl from about ten feet away.

The driver—a willowy, gray-haired woman in jeans and a denim blouse—leaped out of the car. "Oh, no! Are you all right?"

Ron, still unable to speak, looked up and nodded weakly.

"I didn't see you," she fretted. "Oh, I'm so sorry."

"It's okay," he wheezed. "I wasn't looking where I was going. The dog was chasing me. I'll be all right."

"Please, you must come inside. I want to make sure you're not injured." Turning to the dog, she said, "Go home! Get out of here!" The beagle barked before waddling off. "That dog is a menace," the woman claimed. "It belongs to someone who recently moved in down the street. Please come in. I insist."

Once inside, the woman led Ron into the kitchen. "I'll put on some coffee. Then you must try my apple cake. Everyone says it's the best in town. By the way, my name is Ginger Stern."

"I'm Ron Tobin. I live several blocks away. My kids got me to try in-line skating because they thought it would be a good way to shed some of my middle-age flab. I need to exercise more."

"I'm sure you didn't think it would be a contact sport."

Ron chuckled and then winced, holding his ribs. "I'm a little sore, but I'll be fine."

As he munched on Ginger's apple cake, he looked around the kitchen and dining room, which were filled with antiques. "What a beautiful house," he marveled. "It seems like I stepped back in time to the 1800s."

"Thank you. Let me show you around."

When they entered the parlor, Ron let out a whoop and walked up to a large oil portrait of a stiffly posed young sea captain. He was wearing tan pants, a black cutaway coat, and a high-necked white shirt adorned with snowy lace ruffles. His long, angular face was framed by curly black hair and bushy sideburns, which were fashionable in the 1800s. His big brown eyes held a calm, steady gaze. He was holding a large white envelope in his right hand. In the background, a full-masted sailing ship headed out of an inlet.

Ron studied the portrait carefully, paying close attention to the envelope. "May I ask where you got this portrait?"

"It's been in the family for years," answered Ginger.

His gaze still glued to the painting, Ron asked, "Can you tell me anything about it?"

"My grandmother got it from somewhere. All I know is this portrait is supposedly of a sea captain."

"Yes, it's Captain John Fairly. This painting has an amazing story behind it—one filled with tragedy and coincidence."

"How do you know so much about it?"

"You see the name on this envelope?" Ron pointed to the flowing script, which read, *The R. Tobin Co., Providence, Rhode Island*. "The R. Tobin Company was owned by my great-great-great-great-great grandfather, Ronald Tobin. I'm Ronald Tobin the eighth. This painting is part of a favorite family story—a story that begins back in the early 1800s."

"Have some more apple cake," said his intrigued hostess. "I can't let you leave here until you tell me all about it."

"John Fairly was only twenty-three, the youngest captain ever to sail one of the ships owned by Ronald Tobin. John married Lucy Wilson in Providence. Shortly after the wedding, he set sail on a lengthy journey that took him from Rhode Island down the coast, around Florida, and into the Gulf of Mexico to New Orleans. From there, he went across the Atlantic to Europe to deliver a cargo of cotton before returning home.

"At one of his first ports—I think it was Savannah, Georgia—he had his portrait painted as a gift for Lucy during his long absence. John wanted to get it to her as soon as possible, so he put the finished canvas in a metal tube and gave it to a crewman aboard another sailing ship bound for Providence.

"Months later, John returned home but was bitterly disappointed to learn that the portrait had never arrived. Apparently, the other ship sank in a storm, and the portrait was lost with the rest of the cargo.

"Then the War of 1812 erupted between the United States and Great Britain, and English warships blockaded the U.S. coast, crippling the New England shipping trade. John decided to become a privateer—a commander of a ship commissioned in the war to capture other ships. No sooner had he set sail as a privateer than he was captured by the British navy and taken on a prison ship to England.

"During John's imprisonment, Ronald Tobin continued to look after Lucy, making sure she had enough money to live. Finally, after two years in prison, John was freed. He returned home and gave up his career at sea to be with his beloved wife.

"John had planned to have another portrait done, but he never seemed to find the time. He kept promising Lucy he'd give her one. In fact, he had found an artist who would do it. But sadly, John took ill and died before he had his first sitting for the portrait.

"About a year later, Ronald Tobin was in Charleston, South Carolina, when he was accidentally struck by a speeding carriage. He wasn't hurt, but his clothes were soiled and muddy. The driver was very apologetic and invited Ronald into the house, hoping to make amends."

Ginger blushed and laughed. "That's similar to what

happened to you this morning. Except, instead of a speeding carriage, it was a car backing up."

"Yes," said Ron, "but it gets even more coincidental. The man was showing Ronald into the parlor when Ronald saw a portrait of a young sea captain whom he recognized immediately as John Fairly."

"But how could that be?" wondered Ginger. "The portrait sank with the ship."

"That's what Ronald thought. The owner of the painting was a veteran sea merchant. During one of his voyages, his crewmen spotted a tubular tin case floating in the ocean off the coast of South Carolina. They retrieved it. Inside they found a rolled-up canvas portrait of a young sea captain. Because the mailing label had long since washed off, the merchant took it home with him. He noticed that the envelope in the portrait was addressed to R. Tobin Company in Providence, so he sent a letter there, asking if anyone knew anything about the portrait. But apparently the letter never arrived.

"Ronald then pulled out a card that showed that he was indeed the owner of R. Tobin Company. He explained to the merchant how much that portrait would mean to John Fairly's widow and asked if he would sell the painting. But the merchant refused to sell it."

"Oh, how terrible," moaned Ginger.

"No, not really. You see, the merchant took the portrait off the wall and gave it to Ronald, asking him to deliver it in person to Lucy. Ronald did exactly that, thrilling Lucy beyond belief. A young husband's gift to his bride had finally arrived, twelve years after it was lost at sea and two years after his death."

"You told that story so beautifully," Ginger complimented. "But what a bittersweet ending."

"It could be a happier one."

"How?"

"If I could return this portrait to the Fairly family."

"Do you know them?"

Ron shook his head. "I don't know them nor do I know where they live. In fact, I don't know if there are even any descendants of John and Lucy. I just think it would be cool if I, like my great-great-great-great-great grandfather Ronald, were able to return the portrait to the family."

"Yes, that would be nice, I guess," said Ginger in a hesitant voice. "But I am awfully fond of it. Nevertheless, if you can find the family, I am willing to part with it."

"Great. I'll do a genealogical search. Meanwhile, promise me you won't sell this painting or give it away without contacting me first."

"I promise."

Over the next year, Ron spent part of his free time searching historical documents in Providence, looking for clues to any descendants of John and Lucy Fairly. He learned that John and Lucy had a daughter, Ellen, who married Matthew O'Neil, but after tracing two more generations, Ron couldn't find any further information.

He kept up his in-line skating but stayed away from Kimberly Avenue because of that annoying beagle. However, one day, while skating on a nearby street, he saw the dog again and decided to challenge it. *I'm a much faster skater than I was when I first saw that dog last year,* Ron thought. So he yelled at the beagle, "Hey, you! See if you can catch me!"

The dog yelped and howled and tore after Ron, who zoomed down the street and turned the corner onto Kimberly Avenue with enough speed to keep a safe distance from the dog. As they neared a quaint Cape Cod-style house, a middle-aged woman watering her garden called to the dog, "Sparky! Stop! You get over here right now! Bad dog!"

The beagle put on the brakes and trotted back to the house, head down, as the woman scolded him.

Ron felt bad for the dog, so he skated over to the owner. "Don't be too harsh on him," he pleaded. "It was my fault. I challenged him. About a year ago I was skating down the street, and he ran after me, and I slammed into a car . . ."

Ron then launched into a lengthy account of how he met Ginger Stern and saw the portrait of Captain John Fairly.

"What?" exclaimed the woman in disbelief. "You mean to tell me that one of my neighbors owns the lost portrait of John Fairly?"

"You know of the painting?"

"I certainly do. John Fairly is my great-great-great-great grandfather!"

"What an amazing coincidence!"

The woman, Estelle Dixon, led Ron inside her house and showed him a family tree to prove her relationship to John Fairly. She explained that her great grandfather, Martin Douglas, was the last person in the family to own the portrait. But he became senile and gave away his things, including the painting. None of the relatives knew what had happened to it after that.

Convinced of her identity, Ron escorted Estelle over to Ginger Stern's house. Although the women had met before,

Estelle had never been inside Ginger's house. When she cast her eyes on the portrait, she stood in awe and said, "Hello, Captain John Fairly. I'm your great-great-great-great granddaughter."

She turned to Ginger and asked, "How did you get the painting?"

"My grandmother got it from an old man years ago when she lived in Woodstock."

"My great grandfather, Martin Douglas, lived in Woodstock when he became senile and started giving things away," said Estelle.

"Then I guess this portrait belongs to you." Ginger began to lift the painting off the wall.

Ron held up his hands. "Wait, let me hand it to Estelle. My great-great-great-great-great grandfather once returned this portrait to the Fairly family. Now I want to do the same thing."

After taking it off the wall, he handed it to Estelle, saying, "May I present to you the portrait of Captain John Fairly."

"Thank you so much!" Estelle beamed. "I promise it will never leave the family again."

As Estelle carried the portrait out of the house, her beagle, Sparky, began barking. "Maybe we should thank him, too," she told Ron. "If he hadn't chased you the first time, you never would have met Ginger."

"And if he hadn't chased me the second time, I never would've met you."

"Funny how things work out."

"I'm sure Captain Fairly would appreciate the coincidences."

Lost and Found

Twelve-year-old Teryn McGovern knew all about the intriguing things that lay at the bottom of Lake Delacorte—the remains of a circus elephant, a sunken paddlewheeler, even an old Cadillac.

But nothing could compare with what he found during one memorable summer vacation at the lakefront home of his grandparents, Ed and Mary. It happened when he, his fourteen-year-old sister, Tori, and their grandmother were taking turns riding the Buckaroo—an inner tube towed by their speedboat.

Mary—trim, fit, and athletic for a grandmother—loved riding the Buckaroo. But she was grateful that Tori, who was at the wheel, didn't make too many sharp turns. After a couple of trips around the lake, Mary traded places with Teryn.

"You won't last on this run," Tori teased her younger brother.

"Wanna bet?" he challenged her.

"Sure. If you fall off, you have to be my slave for the day. If you stay on from one end of the lake to the other, then I'll be your slave."

"It's a bet!"

Teryn fastened his life jacket and tightened the straps before jumping over the side. He swam out to the Buckaroo and draped his body over the inner tube. "I'm ready whenever you are, Sis."

Tori shoved the throttle forward. The engine roared to life, and the boat sliced through the choppy waters, gaining speed with every second. Turning to her grandmother, Tori yelled, "Hold on, Nana!" Once the boat reached top speed, she turned it to the right, then swung hard to the left.

Meanwhile, behind them, Teryn gritted his teeth as he was whipped to the outside, causing the tow rope to whine from the strain. The centrifugal force was so strong that most of his body slid off the bouncing Buckaroo and spanked the water. He was barely hanging on. His arms felt like they were going to be yanked off his shoulders, but his pride refused to let him give up.

Just when he thought he had survived Tori's most wicked maneuvers, she turned the boat in the other direction. The Buckaroo slapped directly into the side of a big wake and went airborne. Teryn clung to the sides of the inner tube until a gust of wind caught the Buckaroo and flipped it over, knocking him loose. He smacked back into the water, defeated.

"Yes! Yes! Yes!" Tori shouted in triumph after watching her brother's spectacular spill. She turned the boat around and sped over to Teryn, who was treading water not far from the shore.

As Tori put the boat in neutral, Mary stood up and applauded. "That was one of the greatest spills of all time!" she declared. "You deserve a standing ovation."

"It was just a case of bad luck, Nana," Teryn groused. "If the wind hadn't gotten hold of the Buckaroo, I never would've been tossed."

"Slave boy! Slave boy!" Tori cheered. "When we get back, I think I'll have you make my lunch and serve it to me on the deck."

"I don't want to hear about it," muttered Teryn. He took off his life vest and slipped under the water to get away from his sister's mocking. As he came up for air, he spotted a glittery gold object about twenty feet below at the bottom of the lake.

"Hey, there's something down there," he told them. "I'll be right back." He took a deep breath and dove to the rocky bottom. Nestled between a clump of grass and a dark rock was a gold bracelet. He picked it up and rose to the surface.

Holding it above his head, he shouted, "Hey, look what I found!" He swam over to the boat, handed the bracelet to Tori, and climbed in.

"Oh, my gosh!" squealed Tori. "Nana, did you lose this bracelet?"

"No, dear. What makes you think it's mine?"

"You're not going to believe this, but it has your name on it!"

"What? Let me see." Mary fingered the gold bracelet and then looked at her name neatly engraved in script. Her hands began to shake. "Oh, dear. Oh, dear," she mumbled.

"Nana, are you all right?" asked Tori. "You look pale."

"I've just had a flashback in time—forty-one years ago, to be exact. The memory is bittersweet—mostly bitter."

"So the bracelet is yours?" asked Teryn.

"It *was* mine." The tanned grandmother took off her sun

visor and rubbed her hand through her hair. Lost in her own thoughts, she quietly stared at the bracelet.

"Nana, there's a story behind that bracelet, isn't there?" Tori prodded. "Tell us, please?"

Mary smiled and nodded. "Okay, kids, I will. But first, we'd better drop anchor. It's going to take a while to tell."

"Slave boy," ordered Tori, "drop the anchor."

Teryn did what he was told, not because he was willing to be his sister's slave but because he wanted to hear his grandmother's story.

Mary let the bracelet dangle from her fingers. She cleared her throat and recalled, "When I was eighteen and fresh out of high school—before I had ever met your grandfather—I fell in love with a young man named Hale Bowman. He was tall and strong and had thick blond hair. Oh, he was handsome. He was a senior at the University of Wisconsin, studying engineering. He said he loved me, and we talked about getting married. He didn't have much money, because he was a student, so he couldn't afford an engagement ring. But he did buy me a gold bracelet engraved with my name. He called it my pre-engagement bracelet, and he promised to get me a ring as soon as he could. We kept our romance a secret, because my father didn't like him. Besides, I didn't have a real engagement ring, so I couldn't announce our marriage plans to anyone.

"I went to work for my father in his clothing store and saw Hale on the weekends, when he'd come to visit. We talked about the future and how he was going to be an airline pilot and whisk me all over the world. I lived from weekend to weekend just to see him. Naturally, I didn't dare date anyone else, and I couldn't tell my parents why, although they suspected I was in love with Hale. They thought I was foolish, but my heart belonged to Hale.

"As the year went on, however, Hale came home less frequently. Supposedly it was because school was getting harder and required more of his time. By late spring, he was only coming home about once a month.

"Then I heard a terrible rumor that he had been seeing another girl in school, someone named Debbie. I confronted Hale with the story, but he denied it.

"One day close to Graduation Day, he took me out in a rowboat near this very spot. It was a day just like this one, a little choppy, but sunny. Everything seemed perfect. I thought Hale was going to give me an engagement ring. Then he made a big mistake. He accidentally called me Debbie. That's when I knew the rumors were true. I told him my suspicions, but he said I was acting foolish. He gave me some cock-and-bull story about Debbie being his roommate's girlfriend. But I didn't buy it. We got into a big argument, and I gave him a piece of my mind. I called him every nasty name I could think of—and I might have even made up a few, too.

"I thought about deliberately tipping over the rowboat, but I had on my new sundress, so I decided against it. Instead, I took this bracelet off my wrist and hurled it as far as I could into the lake—like this." With a strong arm, Mary flung the bracelet into the water.

"Nana! No!" shouted Tori. "Why did you do that?"

"It brought back a bad memory. Besides, I don't want anything to do with that cad." Mary looked at the spot where the bracelet had hit the water and sunk. "Now it can go back where it belongs. May it stay there forever."

"Nana," Teryn asked, "what happened after your argument?"

"I never saw or spoke to Hale again. I heard he married Debbie and they moved to Minnesota, where he became a pilot for Northwest Airlines."

"Does Papa know about this?" asked Tori.

"Of course, honey. We have no secrets." Mary wiped her hands in a symbolic gesture of washing out the bad memory, then broke out in a big grin. "You know, I really shouldn't be all that angry now. Just think. If I had married Hale, I never would've met your grandfather and married him and had a wonderful life."

"And Dad wouldn't have been born," said Teryn.

"Which means," Tori added, "we wouldn't have been born."

"See all the precious things I never would've had if I had married Hale?" said Mary. "Things always work out for the best." She clapped her hands as if to signal that her story was over. "Let's head back to the house. Tori, I'm sure you're ready for your slave boy to serve you lunch."

"Aw, come on," Teryn complained. "You're not really going to make me be your slave."

"Oh, yes, I am!" Tori declared.

After a lunch of ham-and-cheese sandwiches and iced tea—which Teryn made and served—Tori and Teryn went down to the dock to soak up the sun's rays.

"That was a wild story Nana told, huh, Tori?"

"Yes, but I still wish she hadn't thrown the bracelet back. It has a history. I'd love to have it."

"You want to go back there and try diving for it?"

"Sure, Teryn, I'm up for that."

The two hopped in the boat and motored over to the spot where they thought the bracelet had entered the water. With snorkels, masks, and fins, they made repeated dives, scouring the bottom. But other than two empty soda cans, they found nothing and eventually gave up.

When Teryn and Tori returned to the house, their grandmother was walking back and forth in the sunroom, holding a letter in her hand. Mary had a look of awe on her face.

"I've never believed in fate before," she told them. "But now I have to wonder."

"What are you talking about, Nana?" Tori asked.

"The most remarkable letter came in the mail today. I'm still in shock. I'm holding a letter from—are you ready for this?—Hale Bowman!"

"The guy who gave you the bracelet and broke your heart? No way!"

"Yes! I'm so stunned by it all."

"Well, what does it say?" Tori asked.

"'Dear Mary,'" her grandmother began, "'I hope this letter finds you well. It has been forty-one years since we last saw or spoke to each other, under very unpleasant circumstances for which I am totally to blame.

"'After we went our separate ways, I kept up with your life through occasional conversations with our mutual friend, Beth Kellerman. I learned you married a doctor and had a family. But eventually Beth and I lost touch. I found your address by doing a search on the Internet.

"'The reason for this letter is to tell you—however late this may

125

be—*that I am truly sorry for the pain I caused you. I wish I could blame it on youth. But I was twenty-three, and that's old enough to know right from wrong. You were a sweet, innocent girl, and I was a cheating scoundrel. I can't tell you how many times over the years I was haunted by the thought of the hurt I caused you. You didn't deserve to be treated that way. I can still remember that day on the lake, and it's not a pleasant memory. Perhaps time has been kind to you and has wiped all traces of that moment from your mind.*

"'*On the chance that you do recollect it, I humbly ask that you find it in your heart to forgive me. I know it might seem odd to ask your forgiveness after so many years, but it's something that I need to do now.*

"'*May your life be blessed with health and happiness.*

"'*Yours very truly, Hale Bowman.*

"'*P.S. In case you're interested, my marriage to Debbie didn't work out. However, I later married a wonderful woman, Joan, who gave me three terrific children. I am a retired airline captain and live in Florida near my four grandchildren.*'"

"What an incredible coincidence!" Tori exclaimed. "Teryn finds the bracelet that your old boyfriend gave you, and then on the same day, out of the blue, you get a letter from him. Wow!"

Mary sighed. "Now I wish I hadn't tossed the bracelet back into the water. I wonder if there's any chance—"

"Nana," said Teryn, "we went looking for the bracelet this afternoon. No luck."

"Oh, well. I guess it was meant to be."

*   *   *

126

A week later, Teryn and Tori were fishing from the dock. They had made another bet. The one whose total catch weighed the least had to pull kitchen detail for the rest of their stay. Tori had snagged three bass, while Teryn had caught only two.

"Looks like you're going to lose another bet," Tori gloated. "Come on, we better get back with our catches."

"Not so fast," he countered, holding on to his bending pole. "I've got a big one!" After a few minutes of fighting, Teryn expertly brought the fish to the dock, where Tori got the net and scooped up the catch. It turned out to be a two-pound bass—enough for Teryn to win the bet.

When they returned to the house, the two kids held up their fish and announced, "We've got dinner!"

"Bravo," said Mary, forcing a smile. "That's very nice."

Tori was the first to notice that her grandmother seemed depressed. "Nana, is everything okay?"

"I just received a bit of sad news," Mary replied. "I happened to be talking to an old friend, Beth Kellerman. I had told her about the bracelet and Hale's letter. Well, she had heard through someone else that Hale died a few days ago in Miami from cancer. Apparently, just before he died, he had written to everyone he'd ever wronged and asked for forgiveness, because he wanted to die with a clear conscience. Now I feel really bad that I didn't write back to him or keep that bracelet." Gazing out over the lake, she repeatedly folded and opened Hale's letter. "I harbored resentment toward Hale for forty-one years, and now I realize that all that negative energy was wasted energy."

Mary stuffed the letter in the back pocket of her jeans and

put on a much brighter face. "Well, that's enough of that." She walked over to the kids and took their catch. "So, how do you want your fish? Fried, baked, or grilled?"

"Grilled!"

"You got it! I'll go in the kitchen and fillet them now. Papa and your parents will be delighted with the fish you caught."

While the kids plopped down in the sunroom, Mary placed Teryn's prize bass on the cutting board and slit it open with a knife. She was pulling out the guts when suddenly she uttered a piercing scream.

The kids rushed into the kitchen. "Nana, what is it?"

Mary, wide-eyed and speechless, beckoned them to her side and pointed at the fish with her knife. There, inside its opened belly, lay the gold bracelet!